BELIEVING YOU CAN IS THE FIRST STEP TO ACHIEVING

A CBT and Attribution Retaining Programme to Improve Self-Belief in Students aged 8–12

ALICIA R CHODKIEWICZ
AND CHRISTOPHER BOYLE

Jessica Kingsley *Publishers*
London and Philadelphia

First published in 2015
by Jessica Kingsley Publishers
73 Collier Street
London N1 9BE, UK
and
400 Market Street, Suite 400
Philadelphia, PA 19106, USA

www.jkp.com

Front cover image source: Thinkstock®. The cover image is for illustrative purposes only, and any person featuring is a model.

Library of Congress Cataloging in Publication Data
A CIP catalog record for this book is available from the Library of Congress

British Library Cataloguing in Publication Data
A CIP catalogue record for this book is available from the British Library

ISBN 978 1 84905 625 0
eISBN 978 1 78450 098 6

Printed and bound in Great Britain

'Chodkiewicz and Boyle have produced an evidentially based programme of work that innovatively combines Cognitive Behavioural Therapy and Attribution Retraining to promote positive self-belief in learning. This is a focus frequently neglected by mainstream intervention and reflects the authors' deep experience in education, psychology and academia. Materials within offer adaptability, utility and the opportunity for positive and preventative intervention supporting learner self-efficacy.'

– Dr John Pugh, Principal Psychologist, Educational Psychology Service, St Helens Council

'This is a "must have" for anyone working in educational contexts. Based on sound psychological theories and research evaluations the Believing You Can programme delivers exactly what educators, students and schools as an organisation need. Calling on their vast experience, Chodkiewicz and Boyle have developed an easy-to-implement programme with step-by-step instructions, supplemented with highly engaging materials which address the needs of young people who are at a critical stage in their social and emotional development. This is an "all round" resource which will not only prove invaluable to educational professionals, but also to academics who are involved in the training of teachers and educational psychologists.'

– Prof Stephen Houghton, Director, Centre for Child & Adolescent Related Disorders, The University of Western Australia

'This flexible, innovative and evidence-based programme, underpinned by key psychological theories and models, will prove an invaluable resource for all those striving to engage and support children and young people to recognise their inherent strengths and to develop positive attitudes to learning.'

– Elizabeth N King, Principal Psychologist, South Lanarkshire Council Psychological Services

'Chodkiewicz and Boyle combine positive psychology, CBT and Attribution Retraining techniques to improve academic achievement and wellbeing by changing students' negative and unhelpful thoughts. The programme is evidence-based, endorsed by participants in the 8–12 years age-group, and all materials and resources required to run eight sessions are provided in photocopier-friendly format. I strongly recommend the programme to teachers and psychologists.'

– Prof James Boyle, Director of Postgraduate Professional Training in Educational Psychology, School of Psychological Sciences and Health, University of Strathclyde

'To my knowledge this is the first resource book that combines Attribution Theory, Positive Psychology and Cognitive Behavioural Therapy to produce a programme that has the potential for making a real difference to children's lives. The programme is packed full of ideas, worksheets, resources and materials that will be invaluable to practitioners who are working daily with children who have problems with learning, as well as those with emotional and behavioural difficulties. Indeed, as the authors highlight, the programme has the potential to be beneficial to all children, regardless of any identified difficulty. I thoroughly recommend this book to educational psychologists, teachers and other professionals who are interested in making a positive impact to the lives of children, especially those most in need of support.'

– Dr Fraser Lauchlan, Educational Psychologist, Strathclyde University, owner of Fraser Lauchlan Associates

of related interest

Improving Learning Through Dynamic Assessment
A Practical Classroom Resource
Fraser Lauchlan and Donna Carrigan
ISBN 978 1 84905 373 0
eISBN 978 0 85700 731 5

Cool Connections with Cognitive Behavioural Therapy
Encouraging Self-esteem, Resilience and Well-being in Children and Young People Using CBT Approaches
Laurie Seiler
ISBN 978 1 84310 618 0
eISBN 978 1 84642 765 7

Helping Children to Build Self-Esteem
A Photocopiable Activities Book
2nd edition
Deborah M. Plummer
Illustrated by Alice Harper
ISBN 978 1 84310 488 9
eISBN 978 1 84642 609 4

Starving the Anxiety Gremlin
A Cognitive Behavioural Therapy Workbook on Anxiety Management for Young People
Kate Collins-Donnelly
ISBN 978 1 84905 341 9
eISBN 978 0 85700 673 8

Starving the Anger Gremlin
A Cognitive Behavioural Therapy Workbook on Anger Management for Young People
Kate Collins-Donnelly
ISBN 978 1 84905 286 3
eISBN 978 0 85700 621 9

CONTENTS

PREFACE

Note from the authors

When I (first author) look back on my own schooling, I realise that I was one of the lucky ones. I was a high achiever – a straight A student – who loved learning, was particularly good at maths, and loved new challenges teachers set for me. However, when I began working with children in the area of learning support, I realised that not all children shared my love for learning. For many, learning was a constant struggle that brought with it a lot of frustration and disappointment. As a maths tutor, I often had students, even parents, say to me 'I can't do maths' or 'I don't have a mathematical brain.' Many children and even adults completely shut down when confronted with a task that requires them to use numbers. So what was going on?

What I discovered in my extensive work and research in this area is that negative perceptions of one's own abilities are a strong influencer over whether we succeed or fail. For example, a student who is struggling with his learning, who, despite trying hard, is falling behind in his work and getting low marks, begins to doubt his abilities. As soon as a student begins to doubt himself he loses motivation and ultimately disengages. 'What is the point, I am only going to fail anyway' becomes a common thought. For some children, failure in school can be endemic; it may have gone on for a long time but we have to find areas where students still feel successful and nourish these, even though *the failure* could be deeply buried in some.

One of the challenges that educators and parents face is that students, and by extension human beings as a species, are constantly comparing their own achievements and failures with those around them and are conscious of how others perceive them. So students who see themselves as failing in a school environment may try to protect themselves, either consciously or unconsciously, through self-sabotage. That is, to protect themselves from the fear of shame and the embarrassment of failure in a subject area, they simply do not try. For example, a student may leave his home-learning to the last minute, so that if he does fail there is an excuse as to why. Rather than viewing this behaviour as a student's attempt to protect himself from further shame and embarrassment, we tend to chastise the student for not working hard enough. Recognising that his Perennial Ability Retraction Capacity (PARC) is at play will help us be proactive in attempting to facilitate positive learning for the student. This will thus ensure that children will at least 'have a go' at learning, rather than invoking PARC.

The cycle of negative self-perceptions and self-sabotaging behaviour becomes something of a self-fulfilling prophecy. Fear of failure leads to withdrawal of motivation and effort, resulting in exactly what the student first fears…failure. Through my work with students, I observed that many who were struggling with their learning had internalised very strong negative views of their abilities. and academic instruction alone was not enough to help them improve their learning. For many of these students, learning had been one long struggle; they used PARC to ensure that their self-esteem was protected. For instance, 'I am captain of the football team and I am good at it but in school I am not a good learner because I don't care so I don't try.' This is more acceptable than being labelled as a person who has limited ability by his peers. It is a choice that children can make and PARC assists them in this type of self-protection.

Even before I became an educational psychologist and learnt about attributions, I knew that to help my students I needed to improve their internal dialogue by fostering a belief in them that, despite any negative experiences, they could be capable students. Together with making my lessons fun, I strived to motivate my students to believe in themselves. Being able to facilitate their learning strengths and reversing previous difficulties with how they experienced failure meant that it was possible to see the positive results. Watching as these students began to believe that they could learn was inspiring.

When my path crossed with Dr Chris Boyle (second author) and I learnt about his work in encouraging healthy thinking in students as a way of inspiring fulfilled academic potential, it was a perfect meeting of minds. Much of what we read supported the experiences we had both had working with struggling students, and reaffirmed that there was a real need in our schools for more support in this area. This is how we came to develop the Believing You Can is the First Step to Achieving programme and write this book. We hope it will inform educational practitioners as to how negative thoughts hold students back and can sabotage learning, as well as teach students skills to identify and overcome negative thinking patterns. It is our hope that many of the educators, parents and others involved in working with children and adolescents who read this book think about the thoughts and reasons behind a student's actions instead of labelling them as 'lazy'. It is the authors' hope that, with good adult support, every child who takes part in this programme replaces the phrase 'I can't do it because I am not clever enough' with 'I can do it, if...'

A note about gender used in this book – we have opted for the male pronoun to include both males and females unless an example uses a specific gender.

The programme at a glance

Table 1 Overview of important information about the programme

What topics are covered?	• Understanding the link between thoughts, feelings and actions. • Learning how to identify helpful and unhelpful thinking patterns. • Identifying the 'why' question and learning how to evaluate unhelpful causal attributions. • Developing coping skills to foster adaptive thinking, which can also reverse previously maladaptive thinking patterns.

Is this programme evidence based?	Yes, this programme was based on research findings and has been empirically verified as effective in improving student learning.
What is the appropriate age of students?	• Upper primary years. • Grades 3–6. • Ages 8–12.
What students would benefit from this programme?	All students would benefit.
What group size is recommended?	The programme is appropriate for small (four to seven students) to whole-class groups.
What is the length of the programme?	It is typically eight sessions (but can be modified to between three to fourteen sessions).
How long do sessions last for?	They last approximately 45–60 minutes, if all programme activities are completed. Sessions can be shortened if required.
Who can administer the programme?	Teachers, special education teachers, school/educational psychologists, clinical psychologists.
What do I need to administer this programme?	All the materials needed to administer this programme are provided in this book.
Is the programme interactive?	This programme uses target games, quiz show games, charades, role-plays and more to engage students and create an interactive learning environment.
Why use a workbook?	• It allows for easy and effective running of the programme. • The workbook consolidates the skills learnt through independent practice. • There is the opportunity for student monitoring. • It provides students with a tangible resource that summarises the skills learnt in the programme.
Are there home-learning activities?	Home-learning activities accompany every session.

Summary of what is contained in this resource

This book is essentially targeted at any individual interested in understanding and supporting the cognitive growth and psychological wellbeing of children and adolescents. It will give you a better understanding of your students' thinking styles and behaviours, and give you a new perspective with which to view learners who could benefit from additional support. This book will also equip you with new techniques to support students in overcoming difficulties and inspire the use of positive thinking styles and learning behaviours. This easy-to-follow programme will be an engaging way for you and your students to learn about positive psychology and develop healthy learning patterns.

This book begins with an explanation of the research field and the development of the Believing You Can is the First Step to Achieving programme (referred to as 'Believing You Can' from here on) in easy-to-understand language making the information accessible to all individuals. Topics covered in Section 1 include:

- explaining the important role that students' thoughts, emotions and behaviours play in shaping wellbeing, healthy development and academic achievement
- why all students stand to benefit from positive psychology programmes
- background on two important positive psychology tools being used to support student learning
- details on the development and research supporting the Believing You Can programme.

The second section of this book includes an easy-to-follow programme guide. All readers should make sure to read the 'What you need to know before getting started' chapter of this section, which sets out how to use the session guides to implement the Believing You Can programme. Each session guide begins with the goals of the session, a list of what materials are needed for each session and an outline of the activities. What follows is a detailed description of each activity, how to implement the activity, and links to the corresponding worksheet in the student workbook. Each session is structured with activities occurring in a deliberate and systematic order so as to develop target skills. You are encouraged to follow, as closely as possible, the session guidelines when implementing this programme.

When writing the book we did take into account that no two classes or teachers are the same. Therefore, we saw the need to give you the flexibility to modify or extend the programme to fit the individual needs of your classroom. Section 3 includes ideas and tips for programme administers when needing to tailor the programme. This section also includes a list of further activities and resources that can be used to extend the skills learnt into the everyday classroom after the conclusion of the eight-session programme.

All the important resources you need to run the Believing You Can programme can be found in Section 4. This includes:

- a student workbook
- home-learning worksheets
- extra material.

All of these resources are photocopier friendly, meaning that once you buy this book, you can run the programme over and over again.

SECTION 1

BACKGROUND

WHY ARE STUDENT SUPPORT PROGRAMMES NEEDED?

Parents, teachers, psychologists and other educational practitioners all share a common goal, in that they want to find the most effective ways to support the social, cognitive and academic development of children and young people. Within the schooling system the focus needs to be guided towards understanding the dynamic nature of the learning process. In many cases the student plays an active role in his learning and can only benefit from the learning opportunities provided when making the active choice to learn. There are a variety of factors influencing this decision including:

- motivation to learn
- enjoyment of the learning process
- self-esteem and belief in one's ability to succeed
- thinking style
- resilience
- engagement in the learning activity
- exertion of effort
- time spent mastering the new skill
- dedication to persevere in the face of difficulty.

(Hattie 2009; Wigfield *et al.* 2008)

With the new challenges facing children of the twenty-first century and the increased pressure on students caused by the rise of standardised testing (Hardy and Boyle 2011; Solley 2007), many are asking if our school systems are doing enough to support these elements of learning (Casserly 2012; Lewis 1999) outside the 'practise more and get better' approach. The authors of this book believe that we can do better and by considering how our thinking affects our actions we can attempt to improve curricular results without overdoing the practising. There is more and more research showing the positive impact of psychological and cognitive-based interventions on student motivation (e.g. Martin 2014), self-esteem (e.g. Heyman and Dweck 1998), thinking styles (Toland and Boyle 2008), working memory (Alloway and Copello 2013) and the positive psychology domain (Seligman *et al.* 2009). Notwithstanding that there are many different programmes in the market that target some of the different aspects mentioned, it appears that these may be missing a link needed in our current education system in order to support both academic achievement and overall wellbeing among students (Chodkiewicz and Boyle 2014).

WHO STANDS TO GAIN FROM THE PROGRAMME?

Much of the work around implementing psychological-based interventions to support learning is aimed at students already showing signs of learning difficulties. Of course the spectrum of difficulties can be vast but usually it is based on a recognition that, say, little Chris or wee Alicia aren't doing as well on the tests as they should be. The rationale for this trend seems logical, as students who are constantly struggling in school typically hold low levels of self-esteem, motivation and engagement in the learning process and develop negative thinking styles (Au, Watkins and Hattie 2010; Shmulsky and Gobbo 2007). When we first began developing this programme, we too considered targeting it specifically at students experiencing learning difficulties. However, the more we understood student and teacher needs, the more evident it became to us that all students had the potential to gain from this programme for various reasons. A great aspect of this programme is that it is deliberately straightforward in order to make it accessible to all students and educational practitioners. Some of the reasons that students will be able to gain from the programme are as follows:

- All students have strengths and weaknesses, and therefore all students at different times will experience moments of difficulty. As adults, we will also experience this but we are usually less 'controlled' so we can avoid something we are not good at. Chris avoids that old chestnut of maths because he is not very good at it. As an adult he can do so successfully but at school there was no escape from potential failure and that's where PARC would kick in.
- A student's self-perceptions are not purely based on their abilities, but rather are largely shaped through social comparison (Nagengast and Marsh 2012; Tiedemann and Billmann-Mahecha 2004). That is, even high-achieving students may feel as if they are failing if they see their classmates or close friends achieving at a higher level. In some ways it is about how we attribute achievement to what we've done. The authors of this book, Chris and Alicia, have both worked as school psychologists and observed that perception of success was, indeed, quite often related to the local environment. For example, a score of 16/20 in one school would be regarded as a very respectable outcome whereas in another school it may not. Social comparisons in the local environment can be powerful factors when one attributes success or failure to an assignment mark.
- Student self-perceptions are not always accurate, as students performing highly have been found to hold low self-esteem beliefs regarding their ability. Research has shown that how a student sees himself is actually more powerful than how a

student is actually performing. That is, a student scoring 18/20 who nevertheless believes they are a poor student may still struggle with unhelpful thinking and use negative learning behaviours (Banks and Woolfson 2008; Frederickson and Jacobs 2001).

- The skills taught in psychological-based interventions often have far wider influence than just improving students' learning in schools. Through an understanding of the thinking process, learning to evaluate one's thoughts and developing cognitive coping skills, these programmes have the potential to teach lifelong lessons that will help students overcome the many challenges they may face in their future years of schooling and beyond. Building up resilience to failing is important; in fact we argue strongly that all children should be encouraged to experience some form of failure early in school. By this the authors are suggesting that a properly supported introduction to understanding that *failing is not always a negative.* In fact, it can be experienced in such a way that it will enhance learning capability longer term. The issue is how we learn from some failures; after all failing in some aspects of life is inevitable. We would advocate that, under careful supervision, children are taught how to work with and learn from situations where the results weren't as expected to better prepare students to deal with situations that don't go the way they were envisaged.
- School should be about supporting all students to reach their full academic potential. While a wealth of resources have been poured into supporting struggling students, we often forget to ask if average or high-achieving students have already reached their full potential, or if with the right support they could also improve. Research has been suggesting that every student still has the capacity to grow; findings show that students of all ability levels benefit in some way from educational-based psychological interventions (Hall *et al.* 2004; Perry *et al.* 2010; Toland and Boyle 2008).

In developing this programme and writing this book, it was important for us to design an intervention that is versatile, offering something for every student. While we feel this programme would be extremely beneficial for students experiencing learning difficulties, it will also benefit students with low self-belief, those experiencing social and emotional difficulties, or any student within the current educational system who wants to do better than he is currently.

COGNITIVE BEHAVIOURAL THERAPY

Have you ever noticed that two people faced with the same situation often react differently? Over the past 50 years psychologists have been looking to answer this question, by investigating people's cognitions (known more simply as thoughts). The way we perceive the world, make predictions about the future, experience emotions, respond to situations and live our lives are all influenced by our thoughts (Anderson 2010). This is one of the underlying premises of cognitive behavioural therapy (CBT).

To put it simply:

- first you have a thought
- this thought conjures up an emotion
- together this thought and emotion determine how you will behave.

Let's look at an example. When preparing for a football match, Max has the thought 'I'm good at football', which makes him feel confident and leads to him trying his best and enjoying the football match.

On another day, Max has the thought, 'We will never win this game'. This thought leads Max to feeling pessimistic and defeated before the game even begins. As a result Max does not try very hard and has a miserable time. After all, if you know (or think that you do) that it is going to work out badly, why should you invest any energy in it?

While this idea in itself seems to be something most people would intuitively be aware of, many are unaware of how biases in our thoughts, perceptions and interpretations can negatively impact our lives. As we grow up we begin building a map of the world around us based on our experiences and perceptions, which by adolescence and young adulthood consolidate into a set of core beliefs and thinking patterns. There are many ways that these thought processes are manipulated to distort reality or lie to us (Beyond Blue 2013). This can include predisposing us towards noticing only certain events (i.e. only noticing when a person has made a mistake and not all the times they have been successful), mind reading (thinking you know what another person is really thinking), and prophesising as fact (accepting your own predictions as a certainty), just to name a few. The development of biased and negative thinking styles has been linked to a number of emotional and behavioural problems, such as anxiety and depression. It is not too much of a stretch to see how these maladaptive thinking styles can affect students' learning capabilities.

Cognitive behavioural therapy has a long history and development pattern, which has evolved over many decades. It is now regarded as the gold standard for psychotherapeutic interventions in many countries, including the USA, UK, Canada and Australia, to name but a few. It is outside the scope of this book to go into its historical origins but if the reader is interested then seek out work by Aaron Beck and even that of Albert Ellis. There are many Internet sites and books that will be able to give you a decent overview of the CBT approach. Cognitive behavioural therapy is a form of intervention developed to challenge cognitive misconceptions and encourage adaptive thinking styles (Hopkins 2005). This is achieved through education about the role of thoughts, modelling of adaptive thinking patterns, teaching cognitive coping skills and offering the opportunity for new positive learning. Cognitive behavioural therapy also looks at how elements of reinforcing and discouraging feedback influence the development of thinking and behavioural patterns. CBT has become a popular psychological intervention for treating emotional and psychological problems. Often, however, CBT is administered as a reaction to a problem, as opposed to being used to arm individuals with tools needed to develop healthy thinking styles and overcome adversity before problems arise. We feel that there is great potential in opening up CBT programmes to all students. After all, cognitive behavioural approaches are not particularly new and understanding how we think, feel and act about various situations can be applied to many situations and should not be confined to the psychologist's chair.

In recent years researchers have started investigating the positive effects of using CBT with school students to improve achievement and wellbeing, with promising results (Berkeley, Mastropieri and Scruggs 2011; Toland and Boyle 2008). By developing this programme, and writing this book, we want to give more students the chance to benefit from the positive effects of CBT and to build healthy thinking styles that will benefit them not just on their educational journey but be strong enough to last a lifetime.

ATTRIBUTION THEORY

As outlined in the previous chapter thoughts are powerful and can significantly impact a person's feelings, reactions, expectations, behaviours and future outcomes. Attribution theory looks at understanding the power and impact of a specific type of thought: the *why* question. As human beings we are constantly trying to understand the world around us, and our place within it. As a result we spend our days asking the question *why*. These questions range from the everyday trivialities, such as, 'Why was I late?', reactions to major events, 'Why did that accident occur?', or pondering of a more profound nature, 'Why have I not yet reached my personal goals in life?' Often we are not even consciously aware that we are asking these *why* questions.

Attribution theory takes a closer look at our *why* questions, to understand what attribution we use to explain the causes of events. Bernard Weiner is one of the most prominent theorists acclaimed for his work in developing the current model of attribution theory. Weiner (1985) wrote that there are three levels at which people make causal attributions to answer the question of *why*:

Who caused the event? (Locus of control)
'I was the cause' vs. 'Someone else was the cause'
(Internal vs. External)

Is the event controllable? (Controllability)
'I have complete control' vs. 'I had no control'
(Controllable vs. Uncontrollable)

How stable is this event? (Stability)
'This occurs often for the same reason' vs. 'This was a one-off'
(Stable vs. Unstable)

Weiner (1985) proposed that over time individuals use consistent patterns of causal attributions to explain the occurrence of similar events, which develops into an individual's attribution style.

Attribution theorists have looked to learning as a time when students are regularly experiencing moments of perceived academic failure and success. The reasons a student uses to explain these academic events consequently impacts how that student perceives their own personal abilities, evaluates the merits of hard work and predicts future academic outcomes (Koles and Boyle 2013).

To demonstrate the impact of attributions on the learning process let's look at the example of two students, Amy and Lily. Let's first consider what happens when our two students succeed. When Amy succeeds at a task, such as receiving an A on an assignment, Amy attributes this success to her own hard work. Consequently, Amy has confidence in her ability to achieve high results, is motivated to work hard in the future and expects future success. When Lily experiences the same success she, however, attributes the high grade to the assignment being easy. In this instance Lily does not demonstrate any confidence in her abilities; she is not encouraged to work hard, only expecting future success on tasks that she deems to be easy. Considering attribution responses to academic instances of failure, let's return to Amy. Following a failed test Amy reasons that she failed because she did not really do much study for the test. Amy therefore feels personal responsibility for the failure, but believes that through increased study in the future she has the ability to improve her test performance. Lily, on the other hand, attributes her failure on the test to a lack of ability. Lily sees this result as confirmation of her low skill level. Believing she has no control over her level of ability, Lily feels helpless about the inevitability of future failure, therefore having no motivation to work hard on the next test.

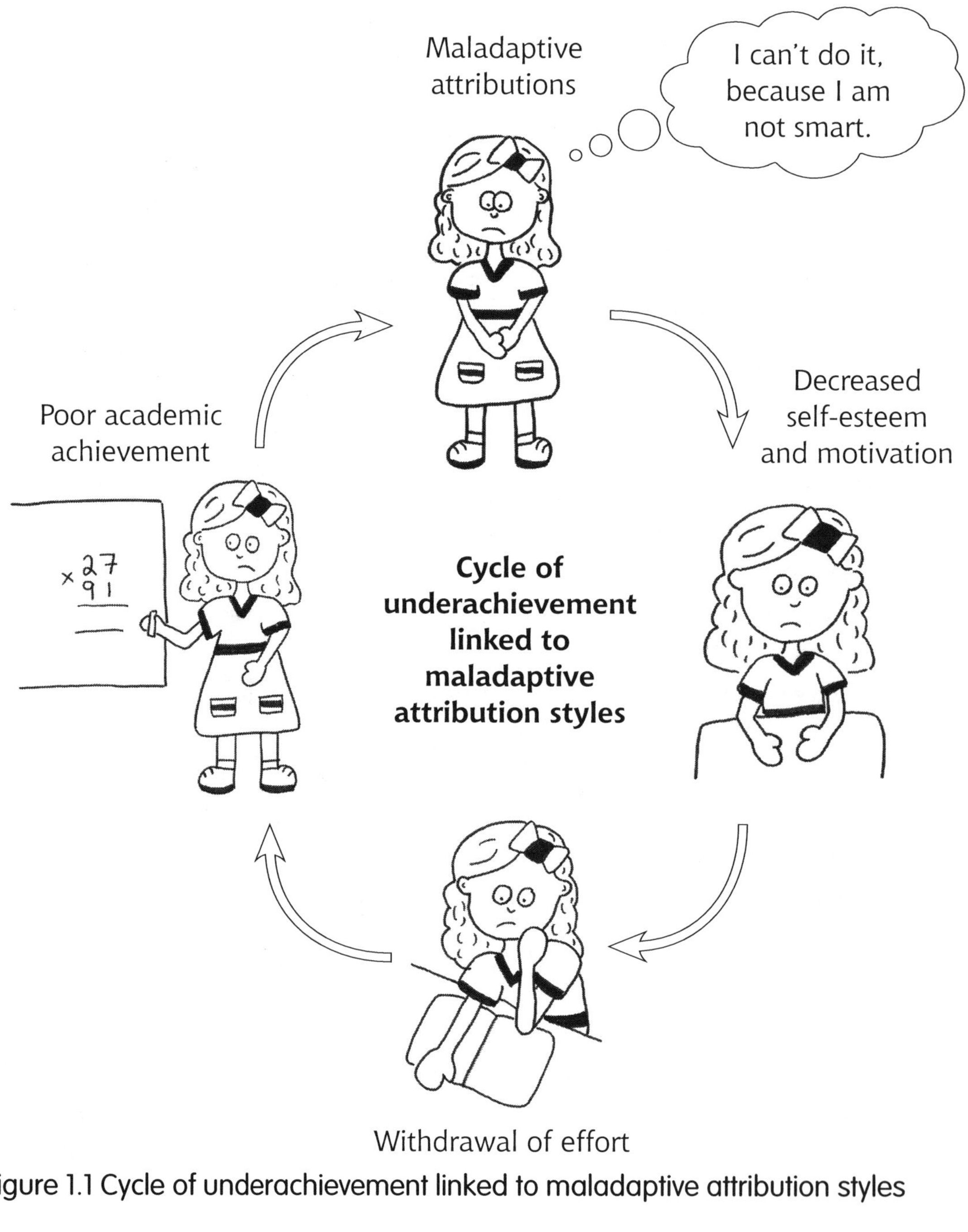

Figure 1.1 Cycle of underachievement linked to maladaptive attribution styles

The example demonstrates how the reasons students use to explain academic success and failure can have a drastic impact on the way they view themselves, their motivation to work hard and their expectations of future outcomes. Attribution theory states that following an occasion of academic success it is advantageous to make causal attributions that assign personal responsibility, controllability and stability (such as ability and hard work) while following occasions of failures, attributions that assign personal responsibility, are controllable and that suggest failure is unstable (such as lack of hard work, or use of the wrong strategy) are beneficial. Such attributions lead students to feel confidence in their abilities and optimistic about the chance of future success and therefore motivated to work towards their goals.

Teachers and parents themselves are often unknowingly shaping students self-perceptions and attribution beliefs each time they provide feedback. While this feedback is generally well intentioned, even seemingly natural responses can negatively shape a student's developing attribution style if it is incongruent with the adaptive attributions described above (Burnett 1997; Perry and Hall 2009).

Attribution theory has redefined the way that many now look at supporting learning and student development. An intervention rooted in attribution theory has shown that working with student thinking patterns to promote positive attribution beliefs can positively influence learning (Chodkiewicz and Boyle 2014). Such interventions, known as attribution retraining, while often not explicitly teaching any academic skills, nonetheless significantly improve students' academic outcomes (Morris 2013; Toland and Boyle 2008).

Improvements in school performance are credited to the associated improvements in self-esteem, motivation, effort exertion and persistence on difficult tasks that are shown to follow the promotion of adaptive attribution styles (Dresel and Haugwitz 2008; Dresel and Ziegler 2006). Research has also found that by simply changing the way we respond to students, by deliberately giving feedback that is in line with adaptive attributions, improvements in student performance and wellbeing are evident (Dresel and Haugwitz 2008; Ziegler and Heller 2000).

Thoughts are a powerful mechanism, and within the learning environment can greatly shape the way in which a student learns and grows. As we have mentioned in previous chapters, PARC can become a real issue for many students and may go unnoticed by many education staff. It is becoming ever more evident that our educational systems need to go beyond the promotion of purely academic based skills, and rather begin to look at how the promotion of positive thinking skills can help students reach their full potential. By drawing on the latest attribution research, programmes such as that detailed in this book aim to offer students a healthier, happier and more successful school experience.

DEVELOPING THE PROGRAMME

The first steps

When designing the Believing You Can programme we decided to use CBT and attribution retraining techniques together. The idea of combining these two techniques was first proposed by Försterling (1985) almost 30 years ago. Försterling recognised the many similarities between the two forms of therapy, as both are looking to change unhelpful behaviours and emotional reactions through changing thinking patterns and building skills to question and analyse thoughts. Since this time, only a few research studies have combined attribution retraining and CBT techniques, with positive results coming out of both the United Kingdom (Toland and Boyle 2008) and North America (Berkeley *et al.* 2011). This earlier research along with a number of other intervention programmes (Seligman 2007; Stallard 2002) inspired the creation of this programme and book.

After extensive reading of the research in the field and using both CBT and attribution retraining techniques in classrooms the following key areas were chosen as important skills to incorporate in the programme:

- understanding the link between thoughts, feelings and actions
- learning how to identify helpful and unhelpful thinking patterns
- identifying the 'why' question and learning how to evaluate unhelpful causal attributions
- developing coping skills to foster adaptive thinking that can also reverse previously maladaptive thinking patterns.

Age of students

Primary school is a crucial time for learning and discovery. During these years, children achieve important cognitive milestones, learn about their place within the world and begin to develop an independent identity. It is in these years that thinking and behavioural patterns begin to emerge. Research looking at thinking styles and attribution beliefs found that the attribution ideas of primary school students often become entrenched when those students reach high school (Chan and Moore 2006). The primary school years may be the optimal time to teach students positive thinking skills, as the thinking styles established in these years have the potential to influence long-term thinking and behaviour. Therefore, it was decided that students in the upper primary years (Grades 3 to 6; students aged between 8–12) would be the focus for this programme.

Making the programme suitable for a young audience

Students learn best when they are engaged in the learning process (Hattie 2009). One of the best ways to engage young students is to make learning *fun*. This programme stands out from previous work in the field because it uses games, and thus enjoyment, to bring together the scientific principles and interactive activities in order to promote positive thinking skills. These activities include: target games, quiz show games, charades, role-plays and more. Each session was designed around the following model: class discussion to introduce a new skill; fun activity to practise using the new skill; and independent activity to consolidate and demonstrate mastery of the new skill (through using the workbook and home-learning sheets).

Why develop the workbook?

There are a number of benefits associated with the use of a programme workbook. For example, the workbook:

- gives a structure to the programme, clearly setting out for students the topics that are being covered
- offers a chance for students to consolidate the skills learnt in class activities through independent practice
- gives students who may otherwise feel uncomfortable or shy in whole-class activities the chance to practise newly learnt skills
- provides an opportunity for programme facilitators to monitor individual students' understanding of the topics and skills
- provides students with a tangible resource that summarises the skills learnt in the programme
- allows for easy and effective replication of the programme (along with this guide) so that it is accessible to a wide range of educational professionals.

Home learning

While many students may see home-learning as the bane of their existence, it is nevertheless an important part of the learning process. When trying to shape students' thinking styles and behavioural patterns, the most effective programmes will be those that provide opportunities for the practice and rehearsal of skills within real-life settings (Hudson and Kendall 2002). For this reason each programme session includes a home-learning sheet. The home-learning activities themselves are simple and should not take long for students to complete. The activities should, however, encourage students to continue thinking about their newly learnt thinking skills between sessions. As with other parts of the programme they are not onerous or a chore for the student but enjoyable and non-challenging, and in the experience of the authors the students actually do the home-learning tasks.

Programme length

When deciding upon the length of the programme, a number of considerations were taken into account. First, an evaluation of similar programmes found that such interventions typically run for between five to twelve sessions with students in our target age group of 8–12 years of age (Berkeley *et al.* 2011; Toland and Boyle 2008). Second, there is often great pressure on schools to fit a range of extracurricular activities into their already full teaching schedules. It was therefore seen as advantageous to design the programme to fit within a single school term, helping the programme to integrate easily into the school calendar. Third, when designing the programme in Australia to be run within a single school term (Australian school terms run for 9–11 weeks) there needed to be some flexibility to work around other common school commitments, such as school camps, athletics carnivals or public holidays. Based on these considerations the project was optimally designed to run for a total of eight weekly sessions, lasting approximately 45–60 minutes in length. The number and pace of the students in the group will influence the overall length of each session. Given that each school is unique, we have designed the programme to be flexible, allowing teachers to split sessions up or concentrate on only core activities to shorten lessions if required (for further details see Section 3).

Group size

This programme was developed as part of a research project looking to answer a very specific research question. As such, the programme was designed for a specific and small population of students and run in small groups of four to seven students. Through the implementation of the programme and extended research, the potential for this programme to have positive effects for a wider range of students has been recognised. There is something in the programme to extend every student, whether it is enhancing the way that a student approaches academic tasks, boosting a student's self-esteem or proactively teaching cognitive coping skills. There is, therefore, potential for the programme to be effectively run with large groups and even whole classrooms (see Section 3 for more details).

How the research helped shape the programme

The best way to develop a fun and engaging programme for young students is to allow it to be shaped by the ideas of the students themselves. A pilot study was used to identify: how well the programme communicates the desired skills; how engaging the activities are for students; and how well the sessions flow. Together with the students many games were modified, new games were created and session structures changed. With each subsequent research project, the programme continued to improve and evolve. The following chapter provides a summary of this research. The programme in its final form should be credited to the inspiration and collaboration of all the students who have participated in the programme so far.

THE RESEARCH

In 2013 Australian primary school students took part in a study investigating the effectiveness of the Believing You Can programme. What follows is an explanation of this study and a brief description of the findings.

For this study students were selected based on signs of maladaptive attribution patterns. A total of 50 grade 5 and 6 students were drawn from primary schools around Melbourne, Australia. These students were aged between 10 years, 2 months and 12 years, 6 months.

Study 1

Students were randomly allocated into two groups, the research group and the control group. Initially, only the research group, made up of 31 students, took part in the programme. A total of six groups were formed, with four to seven students in each group. Measures were taken at three times across the year: before the programme began (April), directly following the programme (July) and two months following (September).

Study 2

Following the completion of Study 1, the students in the control group were invited to take part in a programme being run in October and November of 2013. A total of 13 students took part in this second study. Measures taken at the three time periods before the programme (April, July and September) were compared to student performance directly following the programme (December).

The programme was run within the school day, with students attending weekly sessions of approximately 45–60 minutes. A comprehensive description of this programme can be found in Section 2 of this book.

RESULTS

One of the central aims of the programme was to foster improved academic achievement among students. Academic achievement was measured across the three domains of reading, spelling and mathematics.

Study 1

When comparing the results of students taking part in the programme with their control group peers who did not, the following results were found:

- Reading ability significantly increased for students who completed the programme. The greatest increase in reading skills occurred during the two months following the completion of the programme, when students were able to spend time practising the newly learnt skills.
- Spelling ability showed more improvement for students who completed the programme against the control group, however, this difference did not reach statistical significance.
- Mathematical ability showed no significant signs of difference between the two groups.
- Student self-reported self-esteem showed more improvement for those who completed the programme directly following programme completion; however, this difference did not reach statistical significance.

Study 2

When comparing students' academic performance following the programme to their achievement during the previous six months, the pattern of results supported those seen in Study 1. What is noteworthy, however, is that the changes seen in Study 2 occurred more quickly than was seen in Study 1.

- Reading ability, which showed only minor improvement during the beginning of the year, drastically improved following the programme. This was found to be a statistically significant improvement.
- A slight increase in the rate of improvement of spelling skills was seen following the programme; however, this did not reach the level of statistical significance.
- Mathematical skills did not appear to significantly change as a result of the programme.

- A slight increase in student self-reported self-esteem was seen following the programme; however, this did not reach the level of statistical significance.

The study concluded that there was evidence to show a positive impact on learning and academic achievement. There were potentially two elements of this study that limited our ability to see stronger results.

- First, academic performance was only measured two months following the completion of the programme. While this was enough time to see the positive improvements in reading, potentially students need more time for their newly learnt skills to have the same level of impact on their spelling and mathematic skills.
- Second, different academic skills develop at different speeds due to their varied nature. For example, reading is a skill that students can easily independently practise; all they have to do is pick up a book. Spelling and mathematics, however, are skills that require students to have access to more structured working activities with feedback.

It was therefore concluded that over time and with increased opportunities to independently practise all academic skills, the programme could improve a wider range of academic skills.

The research also suggested that the programme may have a more robust impact on student self-esteem if the ideas and skills learnt in the programme are extended and encouraged within the natural learning environment, as is outlined in Section 3.

STUDENT FEEDBACK

It is easy for us, the creators of the programme, to tell you how great it is. But let's now hear from the students themselves. A total of 39 students voiced their own opinions on the programme; here is what they said.

How students rated the programme

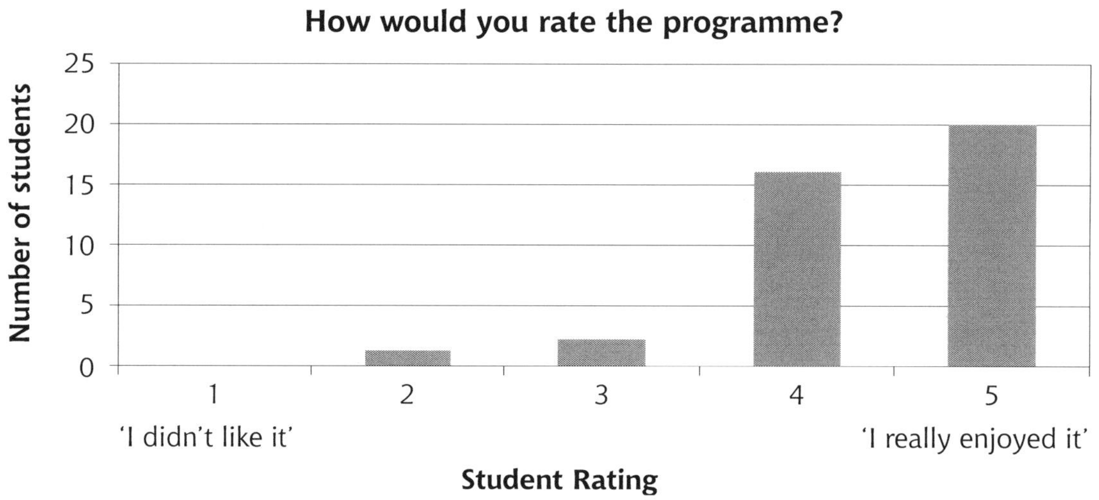

Figure 1.2 Student answers to 'How would you rate the programme?'

When asked how much they liked the programme, 92 per cent of students rated the programme to be four or more out of five (see Figure 1.2). In other words, an overwhelming number of students really enjoyed the programme.

What parts or activities in the programme did you enjoy the most?

When students were asked about their favourite parts of the programme the most popular by far were:

- 'Making a movie' in Session 8
- 'Becoming a super hero' in Sessions 6 and 7

Other popular activities included:

- 'Helpful and unhelpful thoughts targets' in Session 2
- all the games
- role-plays
- learning about being positive
- making comics
- sharing feelings.

What parts or activities did you not enjoy or find boring?

When the students were asked to comment on their least favourite elements of the programme 60 per cent of the students responded with:

'NOTHING'

Only a few students criticised the following areas:

- writing in workbooks
- listening for a long time.

Do you have any suggestions on how to improve the programme in the future?

When students were given the chance to offer their opinion on how to improve the programme, the most frequently advocated changes were:

- for the programme to go on for longer or occur more often
- nothing; they wanted the programme to stay exactly the same
- more games.

SECTION 2

GUIDE TO RUNNING THE PROGRAMME

WHAT YOU NEED TO KNOW BEFORE GETTING STARTED

In this section you will find a detailed description of each session of the Believing You Can programme outlining topics to be covered, materials needed and activities. The intervention has been designed to run as a complete programme, including, in its entirety, the content as outlined in this book. With that said, we appreciate that every student population is unique, and therefore the programme may need to be tailored to better suit the specific needs and characteristics of a student group. In this case please refer to Section 3 where modifications are discussed.

Running the programme

This programme has been designed in a way that allows it to be run with a wide group of students in the upper primary school years, who may vary in regards to their developmental stage, cognitive levels, academic skills and social awareness. When running the programme it is important that instructors aim to engage the students and therefore they will need to tailor their delivery to the students' level. This can be achieved through using relevant language and tailoring examples, games or activities to better meet the needs of the students. The programme incorporates: psycho-education, completing workbook activities based on hypothetical examples, role-playing, games and interactive discussion. This book should be seen as offering a blueprint for how to run the Believing You Can programme, but allow yourself to be flexible to incorporate the ideas and suggestions of students when running games and activities. Most importantly, make sure that you and the students have *fun*, as students show the greatest level of learning when they are engaged in and enjoying the learning process.

Session guides

The Believing You Can programme is designed to be conducted with groups of four or more students. Standard administration of the programme is eight weeks, with sessions typically occurring weekly. When presenting the programme with a group of four to six students, sessions typically run for 45 to 60 minutes. This time may be slightly longer when working with larger groups.This is expected for two reasons, firstly in a larger group there will be more students wanting to share ideas and answer questions. Secondly larger groups of students typically require longer to move between different activities (such as floor discussions and independent work). If you are planning to run the programme with a larger group of students, please refer to the relevant chapter in Section 3.

Each session guide includes: goals of the session; what you need for the session; an outline of the session; and a detailed description of each activity. Sessions typically begin with a class discussion and an introduction of the new topic. Students are then given the chance to develop their understanding of the topic and practise the newly learnt skills through both an activity/game and a worksheet. It is important that each topic is introduced in the order outlined in the session guides and that all focal themes are adequately explained. Instructors are encouraged to read Section 1 of this book to get an understanding of the theories underlying this programme, as well as thoroughly reading through each session guide before administration. While it is important to work through all the worksheets in the workbook, instructors have some flexibility when running the activities. The activities provided in the session guides have been well received by students and help to make the sessions engaging and fun. However, activities can be easily modified, shortened or removed without negatively impacting the programme.

Home-learning

Home-learning is an important part of learning a new skill (Hudson and Kendall 2002). In the Believing You Can programme we refer to home-learning as 'activities to practise what you have learnt' to avoid the negative associations that students may have with the word 'homework'. The practice activities provide students with the chance to independently practise their newly learnt skills within their home and school environments. The practice activities should be explained to the students at the end of each session and the home-learning worksheets distributed. It is often important to provide examples of how to complete the activity or allow students to ask questions. For this reason allow at least five minutes at the end of the session for explaining the practice activity. It is also important that each session begins with a review of the practice activities and a discussion of how students found using the new skill (i.e. 'Was it hard to use the new skill?' and 'Did the new skill help the situation?').

Extra materials

Section 4 in this book provides resources that may help in the administration of the programme. These materials, however, are not mandatory and instructors are encouraged to get creative when sourcing alternative materials or creating their own.

Sticker chart

The sticker chart is an optional element of the programme. The sticker chart can be used as a way to encourage student engagement and the completion of home-learning tasks. A copy of the sticker chart can be found on the first page of the workbook in Section 4. Each student completes his own sticker chart. The sticker chart includes circles labeled with each session, as students can be rewarded for participating in the session by earning a sticker. Students can also be awarded stickers for completion of home-learning tasks and outstanding contributions during activities. Engaged students who regularly complete home-learning tasks may find that they fill up all of the circles before the end of the programme, in that case such a student can continue placing his stickers in another area of his workbook (e.g. front/back cover). To motivate students to want to earn stickers, we ran a prize draw at the end of the programme. The more stickers a student had, the more time his name was entered in the draw. Alternatively you can make sticker goals, where a student receives a reward when he fills the entire sticker chart.

SESSION 1

THOUGHTS–FEELINGS–ACTIONS

Session aims

This introductory session is aimed at showing students how thoughts, feelings and actions are interlinked and demonstrates how changing one's thoughts can have a big impact on feelings and behaviour.

What you need for the session

- Emotion Face Cards (see Section 4, Extra Material)
- Emotion Labels (see Section 4, Extra Material)
- Bluetac, Velcro, magnets or similar

Outline of Session 1

1. Introduction to the programme
2. Make a list of group rules
3. Getting to know you
4. Setting goals
5. Identifying feelings
6. Placing emotions on the spectrum
7. Matching thoughts and feelings
8. The link between thoughts, feelings and actions
9. Activities to practise at home

1.1 Introduction to the programme

The important points to cover in the first address to the students are as follows:

- Explain that the programme is to learn new skills about thoughts and feelings.
- Outline why the students were chosen for the programme (this will be dependent on your selection methods).

- Describe what students can achieve at the end of the programme (for example, being able to use new thinking skills to be more positive and happy learners).
- Emphasise that there are no right or wrong answers in the activities.
- Explain the importance of completing home activities and their sticker chart (optional).
- Provide information about how long the programme will run for.

1.2 Make a list of group rules

Talk through the three rules already in the workbook found in Section 4 at the end of the book. Allow students to brainstorm ideas about other important rules that will foster a happy learning environment as a class, and have each student write the new rules on the lines provided. Try to fill up all the lines in the book. Good examples from past programs include: no put downs, be kind to one another, and don't make fun of others.

GROUP RULES:

- Listen to others when they are talking
- Respect one another
- What is said stays confidential

....

....

....

....

1.3 Getting to know you

This is a fun activity to allow the students and instructor to get to know one another. Each student is asked to write three statements down about themselves in their workbook (Three things about yourself), but only two of these are completely truthful and one is to be an exaggeration or a fib. Each student takes turns in reading out their statements and then the rest of the group guesses which statement is not (completely) true.

1.4 Setting goals

Ask each student to complete their goals for learning in the workbook (Setting Goals for My Learning). Students should be instructed to draw themselves on the staircase to represent where they are with their learning. The first staircase represents where they currently are, and the second one represents where they want to be in the future.

1.5 Identifying feelings

Place the emotion face cards (Section 4, Extra Material) on the board or the wall. As a class, match the emotion labels (Section 4, Extra Material) with the emotion cards (Blu-Tac, Velcro strips and so forth can be used). Emphasise that there are no right or wrong answers; one emotion card could match lots of emotion labels and vice versa. Then ask the students to complete Worksheet 2 (What Am I Feeling?) in their workbook. Encourage discussion about any differences between students' answers.

Many students use a very limited vocabulary when talking about their feelings, typically responding with happy or sad. This activity is both a nice warm up and prompts students to use a wider range of words when talking about their feelings. If a student is struggling to identify his own feelings in future activities or sessions he should be referred back to Worksheet 1 (Setting Goals for My Learning) in his workbook for inspiration.

1.6 Placing emotions on the spectrum

Discuss emotions in terms of whether they make you feel positive or negative, highlighting how some emotions can be stronger then others. Draw a spectrum on the board ranging from 'NEGATIVE → NEUTRAL → POSITIVE'. Invite the students to place the emotions cards along the spectrum. Discuss the results as a group, looking particularly at the emotions placed at the ends of the spectrum.

1.7 Matching thoughts and feelings

Begin this activity by explaining that our feelings do not just come out of nowhere, but are influenced by our thoughts. Go through the example in Worksheet 3 (Matching Thoughts and Feelings) and then, as a class, or individually, get the students to fill out the faces, drawing an appropriate expression each time, and name the emotion that would match each thought on the page.

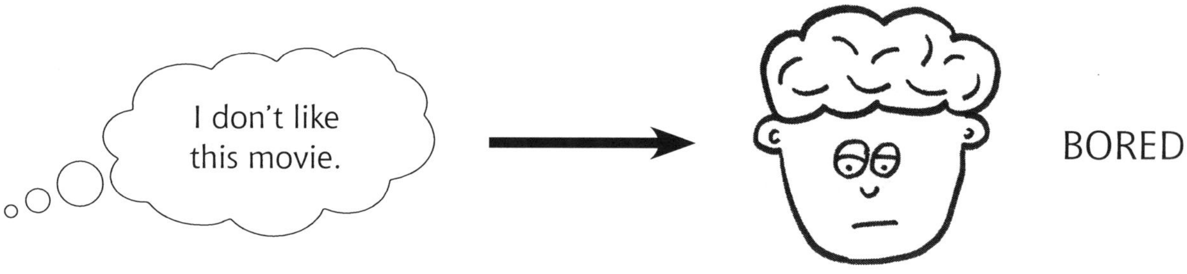

Then ask all the students to put their heads down. The instructor then reads out one of the thoughts from the workbook and asks the students to raise their heads and show, using facial expressions, the emotion that the thought would make them feel.

1.8 The link between thoughts, feelings and actions

This activity is the pivotal component of this session. It extends the previous activity to demonstrate how our thoughts and feelings are important in shaping our behaviour. Demonstrate that there is a pathway between having a thought, the way we feel because of the thought, and then the way we act by reading through the example in Worksheet 4 (Thoughts–Feelings–Actions) in the workbook. Students should then complete the blank pathways on the page, noting that in the last exercise students have to write their own thought.

The pathway: our thoughts cause our feelings, which then make us act in a certain way. Let's have a look at how this works.

Next get the students to act out some of their pathways. Have them first say the thought, show the emotion through a facial expression and act out the behaviour that follows.

1.9 Activities to practise at home

Students are instructed to guess other people's thoughts by applying the thought–feeling–action chain backwards, using the Can You Guess the Thought? worksheet (in Section 4, Home-Learning Worksheets). First, the students need to record an action they have seen someone else (such as a parent, a carer or a friend) do. Then they write down what emotion they thought the person was experiencing, getting clues from facial expressions. Lastly, the students need to imagine a thought that could make the person feel and act that way. The students then ask the person for his real thought and record if the guess was correct.

SESSION 2

HELPFUL AND UNHELPFUL PATHWAYS

Session aims

This session aims to teach students the importance of thoughts by demonstrating how helpful and unhelpful thought pathways can lead to positive and negative behaviour.

What you need for the session

- Thought Pathways printed on half-A4 sheets (see Section 4, Extra Material)
- Helpful Target and Unhelpful Target (see Section 4, Extra Material).
- Bluetac, velcro, magnets or similar
- Scissors
- Glue

Outline of Session 2

1. Review of work from last session and activities practised at home
2. Categorising helpful and unhelpful thought–feelings–action sequences
3. Helpful and unhelpful thoughts targets game
4. The importance of helpful thoughts
5. Activities to practise at home

2.1 Review of work from last session and activities practised at home

Start the session off by asking the students if they enjoyed the first session and revise the topics covered (labelling feelings and the link between thoughts, feelings and actions). Go over the home-learning sheet, allowing students to read examples to the class and have a discussion about what students may have found difficult when trying to guess other people's thoughts.

2.2 Categorising helpful and unhelpful thought–feelings–action sequences

At this stage we begin to look at how some thoughts can be more helpful than others. But what makes something a 'helpful thought'? Helpful thoughts are those that lead to positive emotions and actions that help us achieve our goals and do better in the future. It is also important that helpful thoughts are realistic, as believing falsely that 'I can win every game' will inevitably lead to disappointment. A more helpful thought would be: 'I think I have the ability to win this game, but I can't win all the time and I can still have fun even if I don't win.' Unhelpful thoughts, on the other hand, cause us to feel negative emotions and lead to unhelpful behaviour, such as giving up or missing out on activities. Go through the examples in the workbook, Worksheet 5 (Acting in Helpful and Unhelpful Ways), and ask the students to independently complete Worksheet 6 in the workbook by indicating whether each pathway is helpful or unhelpful.

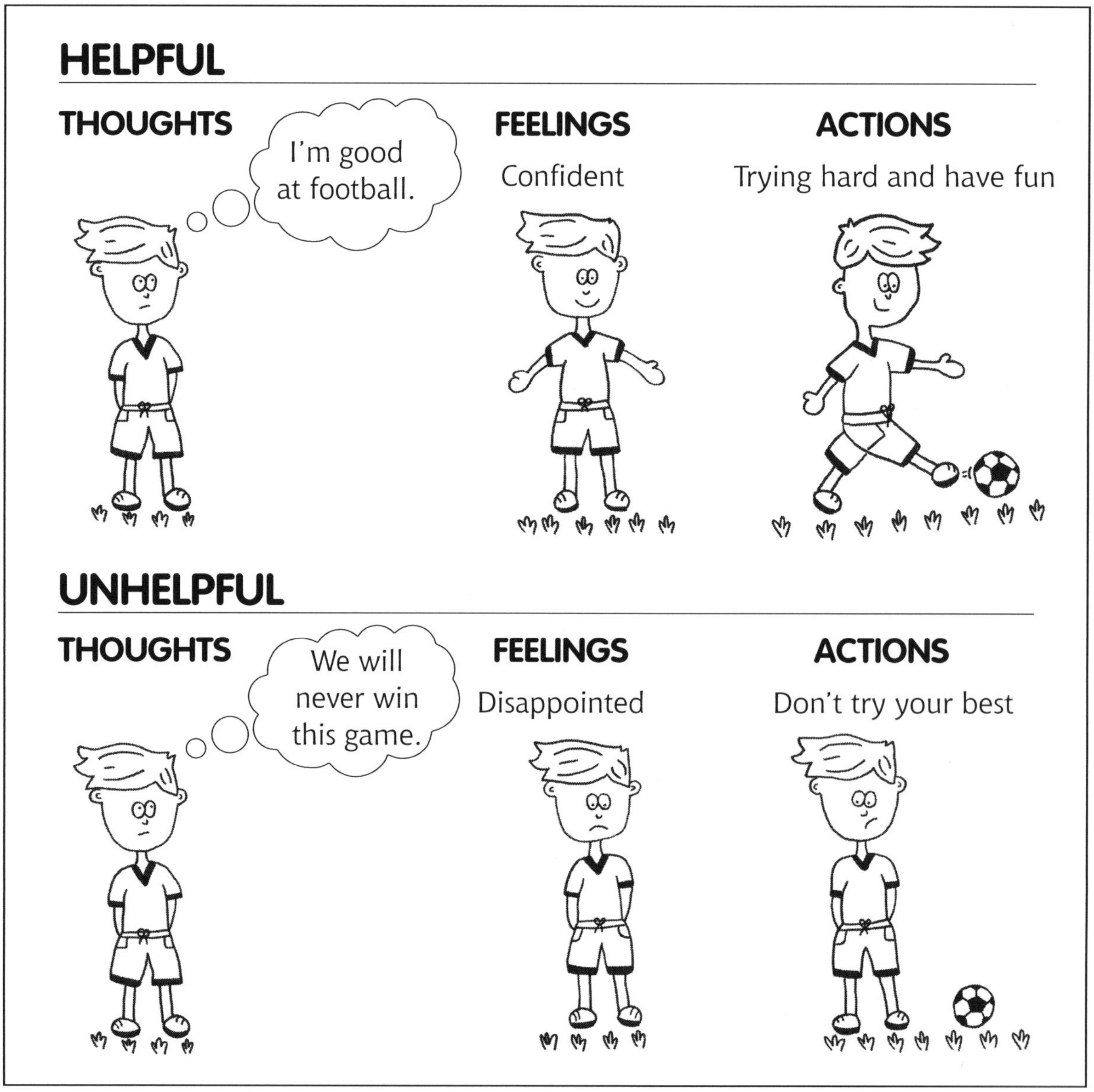

2.3 Helpful and unhelpful thoughts targets game

This activity uses the thought pathways provided in the Extra Materials section in Section 4 and two targets labelled 'helpful thoughts' and 'unhelpful thoughts'. Students form a line, approximately one metre in front of the targets. Each student should read aloud the pathway written on his piece of paper and decide if the pathway is helpful or unhelpful. The student should then scrunch the piece of paper into a ball and throw it at the corresponding target. Each student should have two turns each. Next give each student an A4 piece of paper cut into two parts. On one half the student should write a helpful thought–feelings–action and, on the other, an unhelpful pathway. The instructor then collects these pieces of paper and randomly divides them between the students (making sure that no student receives a pathway they have themselves written). The students are then given the opportunity to play the game again with the new pathways. If desired, students can earn points and the winner of the game can receive a bonus sticker for his sticker chart.

2.4 The importance of *helpful* thoughts

After highlighting the link between helpful thoughts and helpful behaviour, have a discussion on how helpful thoughts may be advantageous. Point out that it is not always easy to think of helpful thoughts, especially when something bad has happened, and that is why it is good to have some helpful thoughts already prepared. Ask the students to cut out the thoughts from Worksheet 7 (Helpful Thoughts) and stick the helpful thoughts in the thought bubbles. Warn the students to watch out, as not all the thoughts are helpful. There will be two empty thought bubbles for students to write in helpful thoughts of their own.

Here is a list of the helpful thoughts students should stick on their helpful thoughts page:

- I have fun even if I don't win.
- I will do better next time.
- I have friends who care about me.
- I have lots of good qualities.
- It is OK to ask for help.
- If I put my mind to it, I can do it.
- I am a good person.

2.5 Activities to practise at home

The activity Is My Thinking Helpful? (Home-Learning Worksheets) gives students the chance to search for thought pathways in their own lives and to practise identifying when helpful and unhelpful thoughts may be leading to helpful and unhelpful consequences. Suggest that the students also try to think of more helpful thoughts to go with their list in Worksheet 7 in the workbook.

SESSION 3

WHERE DO WE HAVE HELPFUL AND UNHELPFUL THOUGHTS?

Session aims

This session aims to help students identify unhelpful thoughts in their own lives and to encourage helpful thoughts in response to success through self-congratulations.

What you need for the session

- A ball (optional)

Outline of Session 3

1. Review of work from last session and activities practised at home
2. Looking at where unhelpful thoughts occur when we learn
3. Helpful/Unhelpful thoughts charades
4. Helpful/Unhelpful thoughts piggy in the middle
5. Promotion of self-congratulations
6. Activities to practise at home

3.1 Review of work from last session and activities practised at home

Start the session by asking the students if they remember the difference between a helpful and an unhelpful thought pathway. Which one is better and why? Go through the home-learning allowing students to share any thought pathways that they have observed since the previous session. Moving onto our list of helpful thoughts, ask if the students can remember some of the helpful thoughts from last week and if anyone has any new helpful thoughts.

3.2 Looking at where unhelpful thoughts occur when we learn

The workbook activity looks at where unhelpful thoughts can occur. With the class brainstorm some places where students have helpful and unhelpful thoughts. Ask the students to think of two places where they personally have unhelpful thoughts and to write those places in the two houses provided in Worksheet 8 (Identifying Where Unhelpful Thoughts Happen). Students then have to identify an unhelpful thought that they may have in that location and replace it with a more helpful thought.

3.3 Helpful/Unhelpful thoughts charades

Play a charades-style game, where students act out (without words) a place and an action where they have a helpful or unhelpful thought, while the rest of the group tries to guess them.

3.4 Helpful/Unhelpful thoughts piggy in the middle

This game uses a similar premise as piggy in the middle, with a circle of students and one in the middle. A ball is thrown from student to student around the circle. The first student with the ball says a location (such as music class), the second student then says an activity that would match this location (such as singing a song), and the third student says an unhelpful thought ('I have a bad voice; everyone else can sing better than me'). The person in the middle then has to replace that thought with a helpful one. If the person in the middle catches the ball the person who threw the ball has to swap with them and go in the middle.

3.5 Promotion of self-congratulations

This activity is encouraging students to take more responsibility and pride in positive events and moments of success. Students are invited to create their own form of self-congratulations and identify three times when it would be appropriate to use it. This is accompanied by a worksheet for students to complete independently Worksheet 9 (Congratulate Yourself). As a class, read out a number of their scenarios, the students responding with their self-congratulations in each instance, for example, 'You completed a really difficult puzzle'.

3.6 Activities to practise at home

The activity Where Do I Have Helpful and Unhelpful Thoughts? (Home-Learning Worksheets, Section 4) asks students to identify unhelpful thoughts in their own lives and report: what the unhelpful thought was (thought), where the unhelpful thought occurred (location) and what the student was doing when he had the thought (event). Students are also given the chance to practise their self-congratulations.

SESSION 4

HOW DOES THIS ALL RELATE TO SCHOOL AND LEARNING?

Session aims

The aim of this session is to demonstrate how the link between thoughts, feelings and behaviours plays a role in how students learn and act at school. The session introduces the concept that thoughts can have a big impact on what students are able to achieve.

What you need for the session

- Difficult puzzle (optional): this can be any activity that is extremely tricky to complete without knowing a secret trick, such as the magic pyramid puzzle (such puzzles can often be found in magic shops)
- Question Cards (see Section 4, Extra Material)
- Story Book: I Love/Hate Maths (see Section 4, Extra Material).

Outline of session 4

1. Review of work from last session and activities practised at home
2. A puzzle to solve
3. Identifying cognitive obstacles to learning
4. Relating thoughts–feelings–action sequence to the school setting
5. Test your thoughts
6. Activities to practise at home

4.1 Review of work from last session and activities practised at home

Ask students to share with the class their home-learning activity, getting them to discuss places that they identified unhelpful thoughts in their own lives. Are there new places from those we spoke about last week? Ask students to share some of their unhelpful thoughts and, as a class, brainstorm some helpful thoughts that could replace them. Discuss whether the students have used their self-congratulations since the last session.

4.2 A puzzle to solve

Use a puzzle such as the 'magic pyramid'. Allow each student to attempt to make the pyramid and verbalise their thoughts; these are often unhelpful thoughts, such as 'I can't do this' or 'This is impossible'. Ask students to verbalise some more helpful thoughts that they could use instead when trying to solve the puzzle, such as 'Maybe I am just using the wrong strategy'. Show the students the secret to solving the puzzle, giving each student a chance to test it out and successfully complete the puzzle. Ask again about the thoughts each student has after being able to complete the puzzle. Use this example to explain to the students that when we are learning a new skill it can seem really difficult or impossible at first, but often all we need is to learn the secret trick of how to do it and with practice we can succeed.

4.3 Identifying cognitive obstacles to learning

We are now looking to link the work we have done in the last three sessions to school and learning. Using the example in Worksheet 10 in the workbook (How Does This All Relate to My Learning?) discuss with the students how our thoughts about a maths problem can impact what we do. Highlight how the helpful pathways lead to more helpful behaviours that help students learn and do better at school.

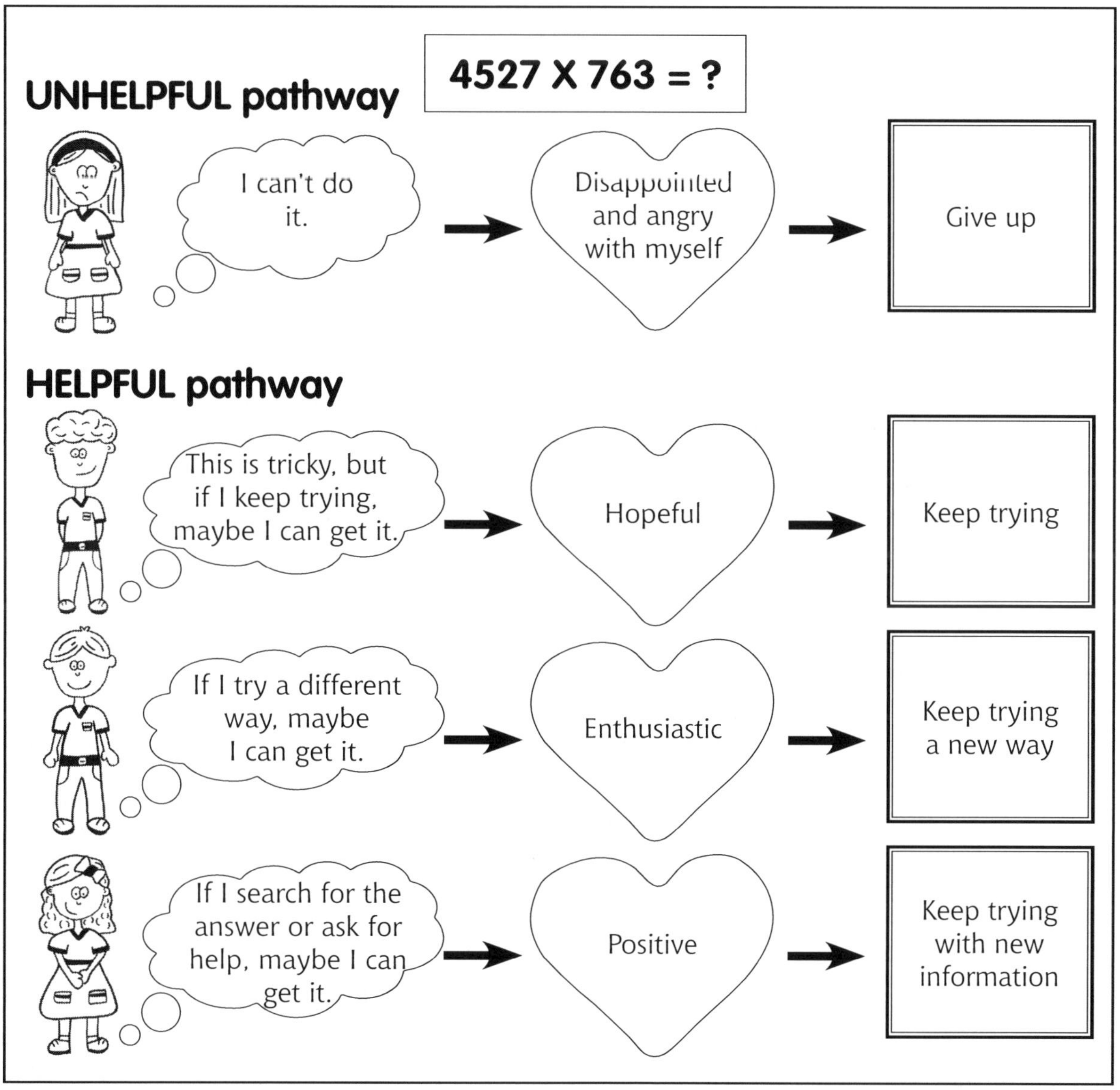

4.4 Relating the thoughts–feelings–actions sequence to the school setting

Ask students to look at the two scenarios presented on in Worksheet 11 of the workbook (Can You Replace These Unhelpful Thoughts with More Helpful Ones?), replacing the unhelpful thoughts with more helpful ones, and writing the feelings and actions that would follow. Ask some students to share their work with the class.

4.5 Test your thoughts

This activity is set up like a quiz. It could be run in the larger group with students selected to answer questions and narrate his thoughts while the rest of the class evaluates the thoughts. The activity could also be run in small groups or pairs, with cards being handed out and students taking it in turns to answer the questions. The question cards in Section 4 (Extra Material) can be used, or instructors can create their own to suit their student population (make sure there is a range of easy, moderate and extremely difficult/ impossible questions). Once a student has provided an answer, ask about the thought that student was having when answering the question. Get the rest of the students in the group to say whether the thought was helpful or unhelpful. If the thought was classified as unhelpful, brainstorm ideas for more helpful thoughts.

It is important to clearly explain to the students before beginning this activity that:

- some questions will be easy, while others will be very difficult
- the aim of this activity is not to see if they can provide correct answers to the questions, but rather to see how they think, so it is OK if they do not know the answer or get questions wrong
- students should not call out the answer or say things such as 'I know the answer' or 'that is easy'; explain how this may make someone feel if they do not know the answer or are finding the question difficult.

4.6 Activities to practise at home

With the class read through the booklet 'I Love/Hate Maths', which can be found in the Extra Material section in Section 4. Discuss how this demonstrates a way to use the helpful and unhelpful thought pathways in school. Invite the students to write their own booklets about thought pathways for home-learning.

SESSION 5

WHY DO WE SUCCEED AND FAIL?

Session aims

This session aims to introduce students to the concepts of attribution theory, promote understanding of helpful and unhelpful explanations for why we may succeed and fail, and encourage helpful attribution styles.

What you need for session

- No additional resources

Outline of session 5

1. Review of work from last session and activities practised at home
2. What is success and failure for you?
3. Identifying *why* we succeed and fail
4. Goodies and baddies
5. Activities to practise at home

5.1 Review of work from last session and activities practised at home

Open the session by asking the students if they can name any of the helpful thoughts identified last lesson when completing the Test Your Thoughts activity. Ask students who completed the home-learning task if they would like to share their books with the class.

5.2 What is success and failure for you?

Explain to the students that when we are learning we constantly experience moments where we feel successful and other moments where we feel like we failed. However, this is not always the same for everyone. To demonstrate this, ask all the students to close their eyes and listen to the scenarios you read out from Worksheet 12 in the workbook (Success and Failure). After each scenario ask the students to raise their hand if they would classify the scenario as either a success or a failure. When all the scenarios have been read out, have a discussion with the students regarding which responses were unanimous and which ones were not.

- I came third in a running race.
- I got half the questions right on a spelling test. This was better than I did last week.
- I finished the maths worksheet, but I was the last in my class to finish.
- I worked really hard on a project and got a C.
- I made a speech in front of the class. It was going really well until I forgot some of the words.
- I was told by the teacher that I was working hard, and other students called me a teacher's pet.
- All the class started their work, but I didn't understand what to do and just gave up.
- I am placed in the middle group for maths.
- My story came fourth in a writing competition.

5.3 Identifying *why* we succeed and fail

Discuss with the students that when we succeed at something, we often think of reasons to explain why we succeeded. Some of these thoughts can be helpful because they make us feel proud and positive and encourage us to keep working hard in the future. Other reasons can be unhelpful, because they do not make us feel good about our achievement, make us believe we can't succeed again or tell us to stop trying. Together as a group go through each of the boxes in Worksheet 13 of the workbook (Success), students putting a tick in each of the boxes with helpful reasons and a large cross through any of the unhelpful reasons. The same activity should be repeated in relation to reasons we use to explain why we fail, completing Worksheet 14 in the workbook (Failure). In this case helpful thoughts identify ways the student can change their behaviour to improve in the future, while unhelpful thoughts are those that make future failure seem inevitable or out of the student's control.

Caution: Many students identify attributions of luck, that is, 'I was lucky' or 'I was unlucky', as a helpful thought; however, they are actually very unhelpful. For example, when a student succeeds and thinks that is because they were lucky, that student does not feel proud of their achievements, as they do not feel personally responsible for the outcome. The student will also feel no personal control over whether or not he will succeed again in the future. Similarly, when a student fails and feels that it was due to bad luck, that student is not identifying ways to improve in the future, as they feel helpless to the uncontrollability of future bad luck.

5.4 Goodies and baddies

This game allows students to test out the idea that some reasons we use to explain why we fail and succeed can be good or bad. For this game a student should be selected to play the 'person', one student to play the 'goodie' and one to play the 'baddie'. The person in the middle reads out one of the scenarios from Worksheet 12 in the workbook (Success and Failure) and says whether they feel a success or a failure. The 'baddie' then uses an unhelpful reason to explain why the event occurred (students can make up reasons of their own or can refer to those in the workbook), at which point the 'person' says how the reason the baddie gave made them feel and how they would later act. Next the 'goodie' uses a helpful reason to explain why the event occurred and the 'person' can again say how they would feel and how they would later act. Students can swap roles for each different scenario. To make it more fun you can allow the students to vote on whether the 'goodie' or the 'baddie' made a more convincing argument, and collect a running tally to see which one wins at the end of the game.

Students should independently complete Worksheet 15 (Why?), by writing one reason to explain why each of the scenarios occurred. Students can make up their own reasons or refer to examples in their workbooks.

5.5 Activities to practise at home

Explain to the students that we are not always aware of our feelings of success and failure. Ask students to complete the home-learning activity Explaining Why You Succeed and Fail (Section 4, Home-Learning Worksheets) by noticing a time before the next session when they feel success and another time when they feel failure. Students should write down what made them feel this way, what thought they had to explain *why* the event occurred, and if that thought was helpful or unhelpful.

SUCCESS

Correct answers for Worksheet 13 in the workbook:

FAILURE

Correct answers for Worksheet 14 in the workbook:

SESSION 6

BECOMING SUPER HEROES – STOPPING UNHELPFUL THOUGHTS

Session aims

This session is looking to teach students skills to overcome unhelpful thoughts in their everyday lives.

What you need for the session

- Superhero emblem (optional); in past programmes students have created superhero badges with their own superhero names

Outline of session 6

1. Review of work from last session and activities practised at home
2. Becoming a Super Hero – introduction
3. Super Power 1: Stop that Thought
4. Super Power 2: Check that Thought
5. Super Power 3: Change that Thought
6. Activities to practise at home

6.1 Review of work from last session and activities practised at home

Begin the session by reminding students that the last lesson looked at reasons to explain why we succeed and fail. Before opening the workbooks ask the students if they can remember any of the helpful reasons to explain success or failure. Follow by asking the students if anyone was able to find examples in their own lives of reasons they used to explain success and failure. If any students identified using unhelpful reasons to explain why events occurred in their own lives, as a class brainstorm more helpful reasons that can be used in the future.

6.2 Becoming a Super Hero – introduction

Start this activity by explaining to the students that while it is important to try to stop unhelpful thoughts, it is not always easy. Therefore, the students are going to learn how to use three very special superpowers to defeat their evil enemy: unhelpful thoughts. This would be a good time to give out or create superhero emblems, and turn to Worksheet 16 in the workbook (Becoming a Superhero).

6.3 Super Power 1: Stop that Thought

The first super power is used to stop unhelpful thoughts. It should be accompanied with the action of raising an open palm to say stop. Go to Worksheet 17 in the workbook (Super Power #1) and read through the comic strip in Worksheet 18 (The Power of Stop That Thought).

6.4 Super Power 2: Check that Thought

The second super power is the most difficult but also possibly the most important and can be accompanied with the gesture of making glasses with your hands. With this power the student checks the reason used to explain why something happened, analyses if this reason is true or false, and identifies different reasons that may better explain the occurrence. Explain that there is often not just one reason why an event occurs, but rather lots of different reasons contribute to an outcome. To demonstrate this, draw a pie chart to find different reasons that could have caused a negative event such as 'we lost the basketball game'. Also discuss how the helpful thoughts from the last lesson in Worksheets 12 and 13 in the workbook would be useful when using Check that Thought. Go to Worksheet 19 in the workbook (Super Power #2) and then read through the comic strip on the following page (The Power of Check That Thought).

6.5 Super Power 3: Change that Thought

The third super power is similar to the activities that have been done in earlier sessions, replacing unhelpful thoughts with more helpful ones. The action to accompany this super power is a thumbs-up. Go to Worksheet 21 in the workbook (Super Power #3) and read through the comic strip on the following page (The Power of Change That Thought).

6.6 Activities to practise at home

This week students are asked to create their own comic strip of a superhero using their powers to defeat unhelpful thoughts (see Comic Strip Story in Section 4, Home-Learning Worksheets). Emphasise that the comic strip should be related to a learning situation. If there is time at the end of the lesson ask the students to complete the comic strip story plan in their home-learning sheet and give them the opportunity to talk through their ideas with the instructor or the class.

THE POWER OF STOP THAT THOUGHT

THE POWER OF CHECK THAT THOUGHT

THE POWER OF CHANGE THAT THOUGHT

SESSION 7

PRACTISING YOUR NEW SUPER POWERS

Session aims

This session is a chance for students to further practise the skills learnt in the last session and apply them to a range of different situations.

What you need for the session

- Props to use in role-play activities, such as school supplies, and superhero capes (optional)

Outline of session 7

1. Review of work from last session and activities practised at home
2. Role-plays: saving others from unhelpful thoughts
3. Role-plays: saving yourself from unhelpful thoughts
4. Defeating the *ALWAYS* and *NEVER* monsters
5. Activities to practise at home

7. 1 Review of work *from last session and activities practised at home*

For this lesson it is optimal to have the workbook already opened to Worksheet 23 (Our Super Powers) when the students arrive. Ask the students to complete the page independently without turning back to previous pages in their workbook. Once each student has completed the page, discuss as a group the answers and what students remember from the last lesson. Ask if any students would like to share the comic strips created for home-learning.

WHAT ARE THE THREE SUPER POWERS?

THAT THOUGHT	THAT THOUGHT	THAT THOUGHT

WHY DO WE HAVE THEM?

WHEN CAN WE USE THEM?

7.2 Role-plays: saving others from unhelpful thoughts

Get the students to pair up. Each pair should have their own unhelpful scenario and thought; this can be chosen from Worksheet 24 (Role-plays: Saving Others from Unhelpful Thoughts), or be made up by the students. The pairs should select one person to play the 'person having the unhelpful thought' and the other to play the 'superhero'. Students should be encouraged to use all three super powers in their plays and can be given extra paper to draw a pie chart with at least three reasons when using Check that Thought would be useful.

- You are learning about fractions in maths, but you just don't understand what a fraction is.

  'I'm just not good at maths and never will be.'

- Your teacher says that the three best students in the class will be given a special treat. You work really hard but you're not chosen.

  'Why should I work hard if the teacher doesn't even notice?'

- Your class goes to the pool; you are the only one who cannot swim.

  'Everyone is going to laugh at me.'

- You come fifth in a running race.

  'I'm so slow.'

- For a project you make a model of Earth. When you bring yours to school you see that your friends' projects are better than yours.

  'My work is never as good as my friends.'

- In maths you can't remember your eight times table.

  'Everyone else can do it. I'm the worst in the class.'

- The music teacher asks you to clap a beat, but you get it wrong.

  'I hate music.'

- Your friends are all reading books that are more difficult than yours.

  'I can't read well and never will.'

7.3 Role-plays: saving yourself from unhelpful thoughts

This is a chance for the students to learn to be their own advocates in defeating unhelpful thoughts. Each student should either think of an unhelpful thought or choose one provided on in Worksheet 25 of the workbook (Role-plays: Saving Yourself from Unhelpful Thoughts). Each student then has to do a short role-play showing the class how they would defeat the unhelpful thought. In this activity students do not have to use all three super powers if they feel that one super power alone will be strong enough to defeat the unhelpful thought.

- The teacher gives you a story to read, but you don't understand some of the words.
- You have to give a speech in front of the class but you are scared.
- In art you are making clay sculptures, but yours breaks.
- Your teacher asks the class a question. You put up your hand but you say the wrong answer.
- On a spelling test you get all of the words wrong.
- You are the only one in your class who has not done the home-learning task.

7.4 Defeating the *always* and *never* monsters

Explain to the students that words such as 'always' and 'never' can be evil and can make our thoughts very unhelpful. For example, 'I always fail and always will' or 'I never win'. Ask the students to think of reasons why these monsters may be unhelpful and what may be the best way to defeat them, and then to complete Worksheet 26 (Defeating the Evil Monsters). Once students have attempted to complete the worksheet independently, discuss how these monsters lie to us in two ways:

- They change the way that we think about our past, by telling us that we always or never did something.
- They try to predict the future by telling us that we will never or always will do something.

Students should be encouraged to use Check that Thought to defeat the two nasty monsters called 'always' and 'never'.

7.5 Activities to practise at home

Now that students have practised using their super powers, tell them that you think they are ready to use them in their own lives. Ask each student to use each of the three super powers before the next lesson and to write down what the unhelpful thought was and how they defeated it (Being a Super Hero in the Real World, Home-Learning Worksheets).

SESSION 8

REVIEW OF WHAT WE HAVE LEARNT

Session aims

This session is a chance for students to look back at all the skills learnt in the programme and consolidate this knowledge through creating a means of presenting their new knowledge to their classmates.

What you need for the session

- Needs for this session will be dependent on the form of presentation that is being used. It is encouraged that this is decided in advance so that the correct material can be available for this session.

Outline of session 8

1. Review of work from last session and activities practised at home
2. Checklist of everything we have learnt in the programme
3. Presentation
4. Setting goals for my learning
5. Certificates

8.1 Review of work from last session and activities practised at home

Ask the students if they enjoyed being superheroes in their own lives. Encourage students to share with the class any experience they've had since the last lesson of using their super powers and how this impacted their thoughts, feelings and actions.

8.2 Checklist of everything we have learnt in the programme

As a class go through each of the points in Worksheet 28 (Everything We Have Learnt). Ask the students to discuss what each point means and what they have learnt about that topic. Get the students to tick each of the points that they can confidently say they now know.

- [ ] How are thoughts, feelings and actions linked?
- [ ] What is the difference between *helpful* and *unhelpful* thoughts?
- [ ] Why are *unhelfpul* thoughts unhelpful?
- [ ] How do our thoughts impact our learning?
- [ ] What should I do if I succeed or do something well?
- [ ] What are some helpful thoughts to explain *why* I did well?
- [ ] What are some helpful thoughts to explain *why* I did not do as well as I would like?
- [ ] Why should I try to defeat the unhelpful thoughts?
- [ ] How can I defeat the unhelpful thoughts?
- [ ] I *can* think *helpful thoughts* and use all these skills to help my learning.

8.3 Presentation

The remainder of the session is dedicated to working together with the students to create a presentation that can be used to teach other students about the skills learnt in the programme. The most successful form of presentation with past groups has been to make a short movie. Other presentation options include: posters to hang in the classroom; role-plays to perform in assembly; or a bulletin to put in the school newsletter. The checklist in Worksheet 27 (Everything We Have Learnt) may be helpful in designing the content of the presentation. During this lesson it is important for the instructor to play a facilitator role, allowing students to use their own ideas to direct the form of the presentation while ensuring that the key elements of the programme are being adequately represented.

8.4 Setting goals for my learning

Before finishing the session, ask each student to complete again their goals for learning at the end of of their workbooks (Setting Goals for My Learning). Students should be instructed to draw themselves on the staircase to represent where they are with their learning. The first staircase represents where they currently are, and the second one represents where they want to be in the future. Students should be encouraged to look back at the first page of their workbooks (Setting Goals for My Learning) and discuss with the group any differences.

8.5 Certificates

At the end of the session, or at a separate time organised with the school, students should be presented with certificates that can be found at the end of the Extra Material in Section 4. Students should also be given their workbooks to take home along with any other material that they have created during the programme.

SECTION 3

MODIFICATIONS AND EXTENSION

TEACHING BY TOPIC

While the programme was initially designed to be administered in its complete form, we are also realistic that it can be difficult for educators to find adequate time in their busy school schedules to administer all eight sessions. When time is limited, educators may prefer to select the sections and activities that target the specific needs of their student population. In Table 3.1 you can find a list to help identify which sections would be best for your students.

Table 3.1 Guide to teaching sessions by topic

Topic	Session/Activities
Teaching students about the links between thoughts, feelings and actions	Session 1 Session 2
Teaching students about the way in which thoughts influence learning	Activity 1.8 from Session 1 Session 2 Session 4
Teaching students about the *why* question and encouraging adaptive attribution styles	Session 5
Teaching students how to use cognitive coping skills	Activity 2.2 from Session 2 Session 6 Session 7

LENGTH OF THE PROGRAMME

The programme was originally designed to be administered for eight sessions running for approximately one hour each. In designing the programme, however, we did recognise that this form of administration schedule may not suit every educational setting. Therefore, the programme was designed in a way that sessions could easily be combined or divided. This gives educators the flexibility to run a programme with fewer sessions, or to modify the programme to run over a longer period with sessions that are shorter in duration. There are many ways that the administration of the programme can be modified, and educators are encouraged to mould the programme to best fit their needs and time restraints. In Tables 3.2 and 3.3 you can find examples illustrating how the programme can be modified.

Table 3.2 Guide to teaching the programme in three sessions

Session	Topics	Activities
Session 1	Links between thoughts, feelings and actions and how this relates to learning	1.5 1.6 1.7 1.8 2.2 2.3
Session 2	Looking at how thoughts influence learning and the *why* question	4.2 4.3 5.2 5.3 5.4
Session 3	Learning cognitive coping skills	6.2 6.3 6.4 6.5 7.2

Table 3.3 Guide to extending the programme to 14 sessions

Session	Topics	Activities
Session 1	Introduction and feelings	1.1–1.6
Session 2	Link between thoughts, feelings and actions	1.7–1.8
Session 3	Identifying helpful/unhelpful thoughts	2.2
Session 4	The importance of helpful thoughts	2.4
Session 5	Identifying where helpful/unhelpful thoughts occur	3.2
Session 6	Self-congratulations	3.5
Session 7	Thoughts when we learn	4.2–4.3
Session 8	Reasons why we succeed	5.2 5.3
Session 9	Reasons why we fail	5.4
Session 10	Super Power – Stop that Thought	6.2–6.3 7.2
Session 11	Super Power – Check that Thought	6.4 7.2
Session 12	Super Power – Change that Thought	6.5 7.2
Session 13	Practising cognitive coping skills	7.3 7.4
Session 14	Review of programme (this can be extended to a number of lessons if desired)	8.1–8.3

One necessary consideration when modifying the administration of the programme is the home-learning tasks. Educators should select the most appropriate home-learning sheet to accompany their modified lessons. Educators are encouraged to be creative and set their own home-learning tasks if they are unable to find an appropriate home-learning sheet to match modified lessons. Alternatively, educators may choose not to set home-learning tasks.

WITH A LARGER GROUP OR WHOLE CLASS

This programme works well with small groups (five to ten students), but we see it as being just as successful when run in larger groups or with a whole class. The whole-group activities and games can be easily modified to accommodate a larger number of students. Table 3.4 provides suggestions of ways to modify specific activities to better accommodate a larger group. When running the programme with a larger group it is important to be aware that sessions may run for longer than indicated.

Table 3.4 Guide to modifying activities for a large group

Activity	Modification ideas for larger groups
2.3	• Students can be given only one thought–feeling–action pathway to throw at the target. • Students can be instructed to write only one thought–feeling–action pathway. This can be either a helpful or an unhelpful thought. • Have a number of targets set up around the room. Have students form small groups to play this activity. Ask students to monitor one another's responses.
4.2	• Have a number of puzzles that can be passed around the students.
7.2	• Students can form small groups (of approximately three to five students) to perform the role-plays. • In the role-play activities, possibly not all students will get a chance to perform in front of the class.
8.3	• It may be advantageous to divide students into smaller groups (approximately four to six people), with each group being given a separate role. • For example, if making a movie each student group can be given a different topic from the list in Worksheet 27 in the workbook (Everything We Have Learnt) that they are responsible for making a short one- to two-minute video about. • For example, if creating posters, student groups can each be responsible for designing a poster targeted at a different audience (other students, parents, teachers, etc.).

Given that many classroom teachers may struggle to find an hour in their busy school schedules to add something extra, there are a number of ways that this programme can be tailored to fit into the timetable. It is well suited to being seamlessly integrated into the school day. One particularly effective method of achieving this would be to make each of the sessions a theme for the week. Instead of running the sessions for one hour weekly, a teacher could run parts of the session across the week, for example doing 10–15-minute activities each day. This way, the programme activities can be more easily fitted into breaks between other scheduled lessons, and may also be advantageous as students get more regular exposure to the material.

ENCOURAGING STUDENTS TO USE THE SKILLS IN THEIR OWN LIVES

The programme was designed so that it could be effectively implemented both within a school setting and externally, as well as allowing for a range of educational professionals to fill the role of instructor. The research so far has shown the programme to be effective when run outside of the classroom by an independent person (school psychologist). However, we believe that the programme will be most effective when the ideas and skills learnt are integrated into students' everyday lives. Therefore, where possible, teachers and parents are encouraged to model the positive-thinking patterns outlined in the programme and to prompt students to use the newly learnt coping skills. What follows is a list of examples of ways in which teachers and parents can integrate the programme skills into the everyday.

Understanding actions

When a child engages in a negative behaviour, such as hitting another student or refusing to do an activity, a typical response is to ask that student why they engaged in such behaviour. Students, however, often find it difficult to articulate the reasons behind their actions. Alternatively, teachers and parents can use the vocabulary and skills taught in the programme to ask questions to prompt a student to identify the root thought underlying their behaviour. Refer to the Understanding Actions sheet (Extra Material found in Section 4), which students can complete individually.

Evaluating thoughts

Students should be encouraged to identify their thoughts as either:

A poster to display in the classroom can be found in Section 4.

The best way for you to encourage the use of this vocabulary to evaluate thoughts is to use helpful thoughts yourself. For example: 'I am thinking that our class is going to perform well at assembly today. That is a very helpful thought.'

Encouraging helpful thoughts

If a student is having an unhelpful thought or is showing signs of low motivation, encourage that student to think of a more helpful thought. Students struggling to think of helpful thoughts can be referred to Worksheet 7 (Helpful Thoughts) and Worksheet 10 (How Does This All Relate to My Learning?) in the workbook for some hints and ideas. A Helpful Thoughts Poster can also be found in the Extra Material section in Section 4 or one can be made by the students and displayed around the classroom.

Using self-congratulations

Students should be encouraged as much as possible to be proud of their achievements. In session 3 students created their own form of self-congratulations expression. It is encouraged that each student in the class, or each person in a family, should have a form of expression to congratulate himself. The self-congratulations can be different for each student or the class can decide on one together. Following a moment of success, be it big or small, students should be encouraged to use their self-congratulations. The best way you can encourage students to do this is to model the behaviour yourself, so go on and congratulate yourself.

Explaining why?

One of the key aims of the programme is to prompt students to think about the reasons they use to explain moments of success and failure, as well as to highlight how these explanations can be helpful or unhelpful. At times when students are likely to experience feelings of success and failure (such as following class presentations or when receiving the results of a test) it would be valuable for teachers and parents to prompt students to think about their *why* explanations. This can be a verbal prompt or an individually completed sheet (refer to the Explaining Why? sheet in Section 4). Students should then be encouraged to evaluate their reasons, and replace any unhelpful explanations with more helpful ones. Students should be directed to Worksheet 13 (Success) and Worksheet 14 (Failure) in the workbook if they are having difficulty with this.

Modelling adaptive attributions

The best way to encourage students to use helpful reasons in moments of success and failure is to provide them with attribution-congruent feedback. That is, instead of just giving a student praise, for example, 'good job', include a positive *why* statement: 'I noticed that you worked hard on that picture and it looks great – good job.' Research has shown that modelling of adaptive attributions through teacher feedback can be an effective way of fostering improved thinking styles and academic achievement among students (Perry and Hall 2009). The following are some ideas for feedback responses that can be used to model adaptive attributions.

Praising success

- You really worked hard/put in a lot of effort.
- You are really good at _______.
- When you had a problem, you didn't give up.
- When you had a problem, you asked someone for help and together you were able to find the answer.
- You used the right strategy.

Responding to difficulty and failure

- You only tried one strategy to solve the problem. Maybe next time if you try different strategies you can get it.
- Next time if you try a little harder maybe you can get it.
- You gave up too quickly when you had a problem. Next time, if you keep trying even when it becomes difficult, you may get it.
- You didn't ask for help when you had a problem. Maybe next time if you ask for help we can work it out together.

Using cognitive coping strategies

When students are having unhelpful thoughts encourage them to use the three super powers learnt in the programme. A recap of the three super powers:

STOP that THOUGHT: where students are instructed to stop the unhelpful thought in its tracks

CHECK that THOUGHT: where students check to see if their thoughts are really telling the truth

CHANGE that THOUGHT: where students replace the thought with a more helpful one.

A Super Powers Poster to display in the classroom can be found in Section 4 (Extra Material).

Independent practice

Research suggested that the programme has the most effective impact on learning when a student has the chance to independently practise an academic skill. It was found that while reading is a skill that can be easily independently practised, as most students have access to books, other academic skills such as mathematics and spelling are less often practised outside of the classroom. One of the ways that the programme is expected to improve academic performance is by increasing student motivation to work hard toward their goals. It is anticipated therefore that students following the programme will be more likely to complete voluntary learning activities. Additional work can be provided for students in the form of non-compulsory worksheets or online learning games that students can complete when they finish work early in class, have free time or are at home.

Review of the programme

The programme will be most effective in the long term if material is regularly reviewed and discussed. For example, at the beginning of each school term teachers can discuss with the students what was learnt in the programme and how the positive-thinking skills can be used to help their learning. At the end of each school term, teachers can again discuss with the students the elements of the programme that they tried to implement during the term, and to evaluate which elements they found helpful. As students develop and learning challenges change, it may be helpful to give students a chance to brainstorm some new helpful thoughts or create alternative super powers.

REFERENCES

Alloway, T.P. and Copello, E. (2013) 'Working memory: The what, the why, and the how.' *The Australian Educational and Developmental Psychologist 30*, 2, 105–118.

Anderson, J. (2010) *Cognitive Psychology and its Implications.* New York: Worth Publishers.

Au, R., Watkins, D. and Hattie, J. (2010) 'Academic risk factors and deficits of learned hopelessness: A longitudinal study of Hong Kong secondary school students.' *Educational Psychology 30*, 2, 125–138.

Banks, M. and Woolfson, L. (2008) 'Why do students think they fail? The relationship between attributions and academic self-perceptions.' *British Journal of Special Education 35*, 1, 49–56.

Berkeley, S., Mastropieri, M. and Scruggs, T. (2011) 'Reading comprehension strategies for secondary students with learning and other mild disabilities.' *Journal of Learning Disabilities 44*, 1, 18–32.

Beyond Blue (2013) Common Thinking Errors (handout). Available at www.beyondblue.org.au/docs/default-source/senseability/common-thinking-errors.pdf?sfvrsn=2, accessed on 21 August 2013.

Burnett, P. (1997) 'Children's self-talk and academic self-concept.' *Educational Psychology in Practice 15*, 3, 195–200.

Casserly, A.M. (2012) 'The socio-emotional needs of children with dyslexia in different educational settings in Ireland.' *Journal of Research in Special Educational Needs*, doi:10.1111/j.1471-3802.2011.01227.x.

Chan, L. and Moore, P. (2006) 'Development of attributional beliefs and strategic knowledge in Years 5–9: A longitudinal analysis.' *Educational Psychology 26*, 2, 161–185.

Chodkiewicz, A.R. and Boyle, C. (2014) 'Exploring the contribution of attribution retraining to student perceptions and the learning process.' *Educational Psychology in Practice 30*, 1, 78–87.

Dresel, M. and Haugwitz, M. (2008) 'A computer-based approach to fostering motivation and self-regulated learning.' *The Journal of Experimental Education 77*, 1, 3–18.

Dresel, M. and Ziegler, A. (2006) 'Langfristige Förderung von Fähigkeitsselbstkonzept und impliziter Fähigkeitstheorie durch computerbasiertes attributionales Feedback.' *Zeitschrift für Pädagogische Psychologie 20*, 1, 49–63.

Försterling, F. (1985) 'Attribution retraining: A review.' *Psychological Bulletin 98*, 3, 495–512.

Frederickson, N. and Jacobs, S. (2001) 'Controllability attributions for academic performance and the perceived scholastic competence, global self-worth and achievement of children with dyslexia.' *School Psychology International 22*, 4, 401–416.

Hall, N., Hladkyj, S., Perry, R. and Ruthig, J. (2004) 'The role of attribution retraining and elaborative learning in college students' academic development.' *The Journal of Social Psychology 144*, 6, 591–612.

Hardy, I. and Boyle, C. (2011) 'My school? Critiquing the abstraction and quantification of education.' *Asia-Pacific Journal of Teacher Education 39*, 3, 211–222.

Hattie, J. (2009) *Visible Learning: A Synthesis of Over 800 Meta-analyses Relating to Achievement.* Abingdon: Routledge.

Heyman, G.D. and Dweck, C.S. (1998) 'Children's thinking about traits: Implications for judgments of the self and others.' *Child Development 64,* 2, 391–403.

Hopkins, B. (2005) *The Cambridge Encyclopedia of Child Development.* Cambridge: Cambridge University Press.

Hudson, J. and Kendall, P. (2002) 'Showing you can do it: homework in therapy for children and adolescents with anxiety disorder.' *Psychotherapy in Practice 58,* 5, 525–534.

Koles, J. and Boyle, C. (2013) 'Future Directions of Attribution Retraining for Students with Learning Difficulties: A Review.' In C. Boyle (ed.) *Student Learning: Improving Practice.* New York: Nova Publishers.

Lewis, J. (1999) 'Research into the concept of resilience as a basis for the curriculum for children with EBD.' *Emotional and Behavioural Difficulties 4,* 2, 11–22.

Martin, A.J. (2014) 'Motivation to Learn.' In A. Holliman (ed.) *The Routledge International Companion to Educational Psychology.* London: Routledge.

Morris, M. (2013) 'A naturalistic investigation into the effectiveness of an attribution retraining programme for academic performance.' *Social Sciences Directory 2,* 2, 16–30.

Nagengast, B. and Marsh, H. (2012) 'Big fish in little ponds aspire more: Mediation and cross-cultural generalizability of school-average ability effects on self-concept and career aspirations in science.' *Journal of Educational Psychology 104,* 4, 1033–1053.

Perry, R. and Hall, N. (2009) 'Attribution Retraining in Academic Achievement Settings.' In E. Anderman and L. Anderman (eds) *The Psychology of Classroom Learning: An Encyclopaedia.* New Jersey, NJ: Thomson Gale Publishers.

Perry, R., Stupnisky, R., Hall, N., Chipperfield, J. and Weiner, B. (2010) 'Bad starts and better finishes: Attributional retraining and initial performance in competitive achievement settings.' *Journal of Social and Clinical Psychology 29,* 6, 668–700.

Seligman, M. (2007) *The Optimistic Child: A Proven Program to Safeguard Children Against Depression and Build Lifelong Resilience.* New York: Houghton Mifflin.

Seligman, M.E.P., Ernst, R.M., Gillham, J., Reivich, K. and Linkins, M. (2009) 'Positive education: Positive psychology and classroom interventions.' *Oxford Review of Education 35,* 3, 293–311.

Shmulsky, S. and Gobbo, K. (2007) 'Explanatory style and college students with ADHD and LD.' *Journal of Attention Disorders 10,* 3, 299–305.

Solley, B. (2007) 'On standardized testing: An ACEI position paper.' *Childhood Education 84,* 1, 31–37.

Stallard, P. (2002) *Think Good – Feel Good: A Cognitive Behaviour Therapy Workbook for Children and Young People.* Chichester: John Wiley and Sons.

Tiedemann, J. and Billmann-Mahecha, E. (2004) Development of self-concept in elementary school classes: A test of theoretical models. Available at www.self.ox.ac.uk/Conferences/2004_Tiedemann_Billmann-Manecha.pdf, accessed on 16 March 2015.

Toland, J. and Boyle, C. (2008) 'Applying cognitive behavioural methods to retraining children's attribution for success and failure in learning.' *School Psychology International 29,* 3, 286–302.

Weiner, B. (1985) 'An attributional theory of achievement motivation and emotion.' *Psychological Review 92,* 4, 548–573.

Wigfield, A., Eccles, J.S., Schiefele, U. and Roeser, R. (2008) 'Development of Achievement Motivation.' In W. Damon and R.M. Lerner (eds) *Child and Adolescent Development: An Advanced Course.* New York: Wiley.

Ziegler, A. and Heller, K.A. (2000) 'Effect of an attribution retraining with female students gifted in physics.' *Journal of the Education of the Gifted 23,* 2, 217–243.

SECTION 4

PROGRAMME RESOURCES

LIST OF PROGRAMME RESOURCES

Home-Learning Worksheets

Can You Guess the Thought?

Is My Thinking Helpful?

Where Do I Have Helpful and Unhelpful Thoughts?

Making a Book About Helpful Thinking

Explaining Why You Succeed and Fail

Comic Strip Story

Being a Superhero in the Real World

Extra Material

Emotion Face Cards

Emotion Labels

Thought Pathways

Helpful Target

Unhelpful Target

Question Cards

Story Book

Understanding Actions

Evaluating Thoughts Poster

Helpful Thoughts Poster

Explaining *Why*?

Super Powers Poster

Certificate

WORKBOOK

BELIEVING YOU CAN IS THE FIRST STEP TO ACHIEVING

THIS WORKBOOK BELONGS TO: ______________________________

I AM IN CLASS: ______________________________

AT SCHOOL: ______________________________

HERE IS A PICTURE OF ME:

MY STICKER CHART

Session 1

Session 5

Session 3

Session 4

Session 2

Session 7

Session 6

Session 8

GROUP RULES:

- ➪ Listen to others when they are talking
- ➪ Respect one another
- ➪ What is said stays confidential

✎ ....

✎ ....

✎ ....

✎ ....

THREE THINGS ABOUT YOURSELF:

(one is not true or is an exaggeration)

✎ ....

✎ ....

✎ ....

1. SETTING GOALS FOR MY LEARNING

Where do you think you are *now* with your achievements at school?

Draw yourself on the staircase.

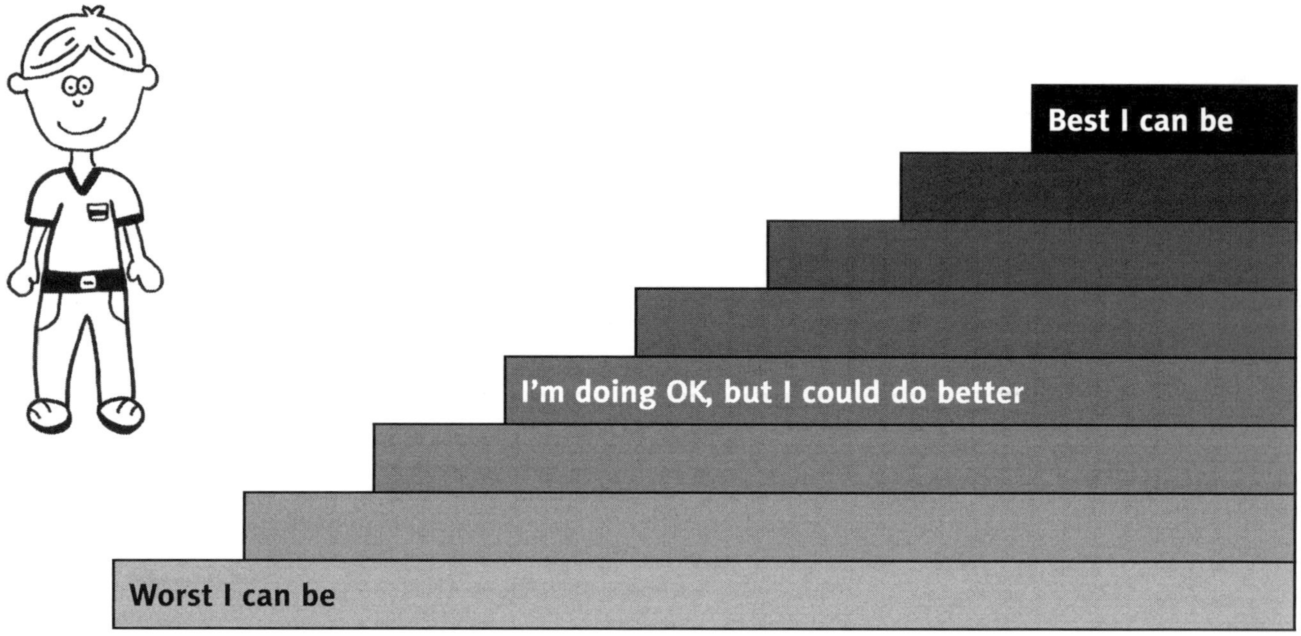

Where do you *want to be* with your achievements at school?

Draw yourself on the staircase.

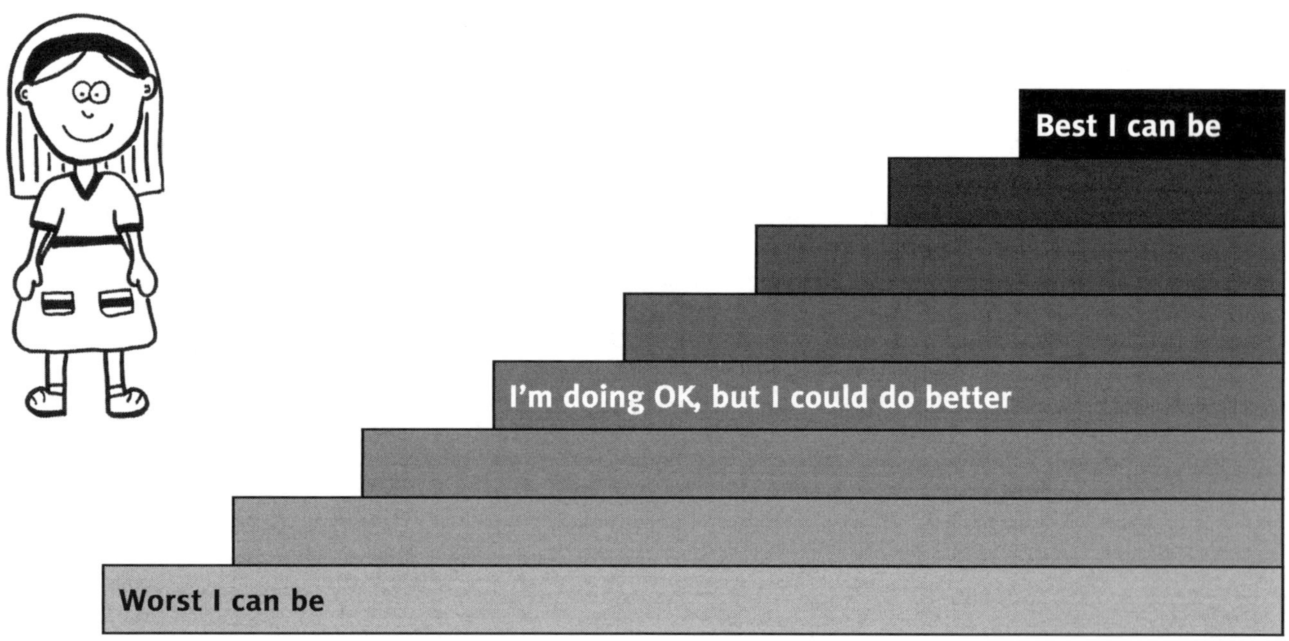

2. WHAT AM I FEELING?

Write the *emotion* shown in each picture using these emotion labels:

Hopeful	Sad	Confident	Angry	Anxious
Surprised	Frustrated	Bored	Disgusted	Happy

3. MATCHING THOUGHTS AND FEELINGS

Our thoughts influence how we feel. It is important to know which thoughts make us feel what feelings.

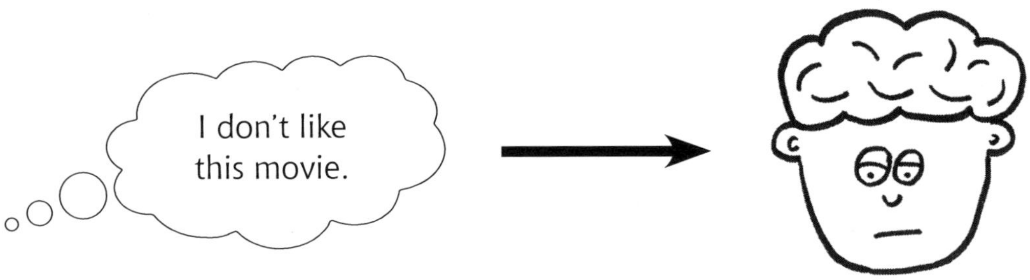

BORED

Let's see how these thoughts may make someone feel.

THOUGHTS | **FEELINGS**

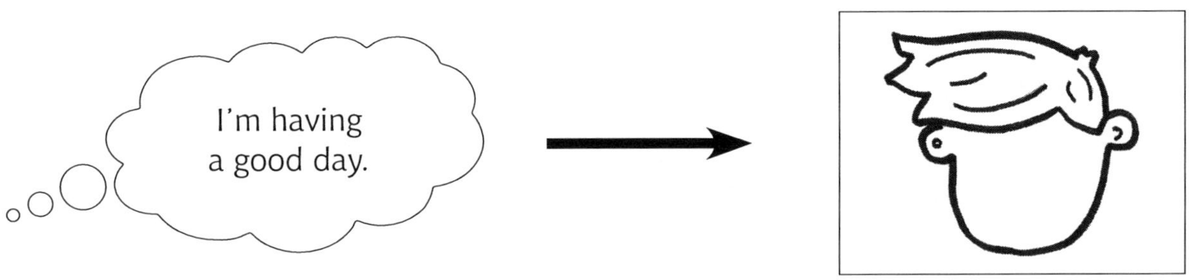

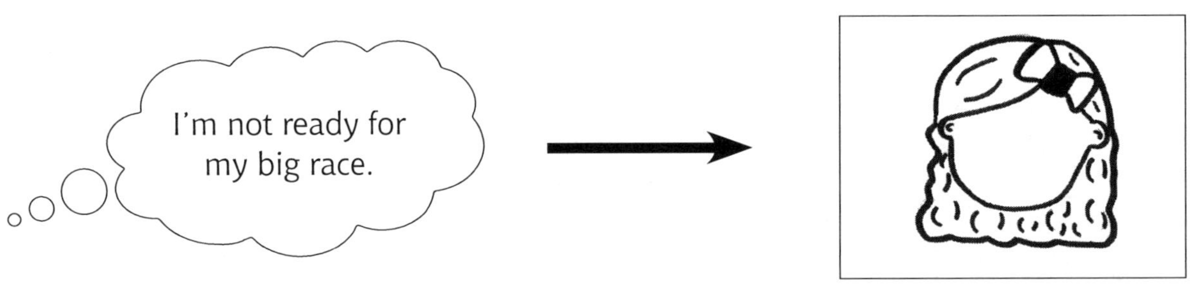

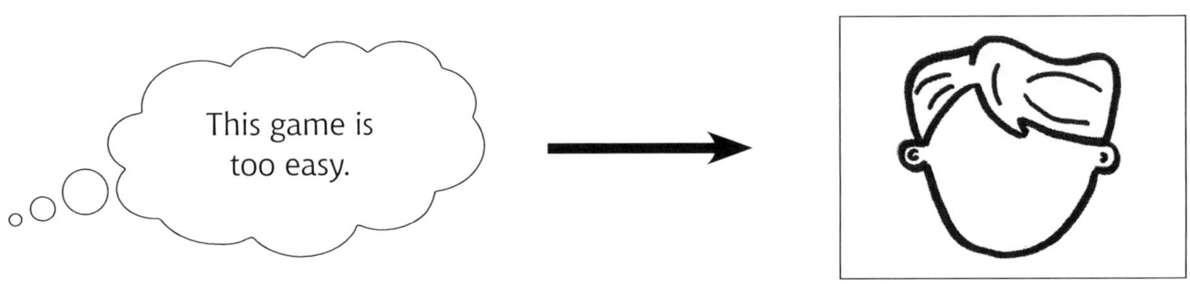

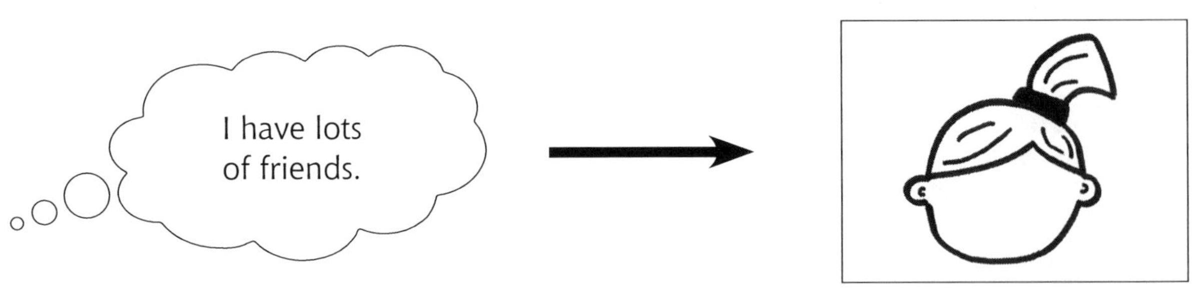

4. THOUGHTS–FEELINGS–ACTIONS

The pathway: our thoughts cause our feelings, which then make us act in a certain way. Let's have a look at how this works.

THOUGHTS

FEELINGS

Excited

ACTIONS

Paint a picture and have fun.

Complete the pathways by drawing the facial expression of how a person would feel after having the thought given, and then write the action that they would do.

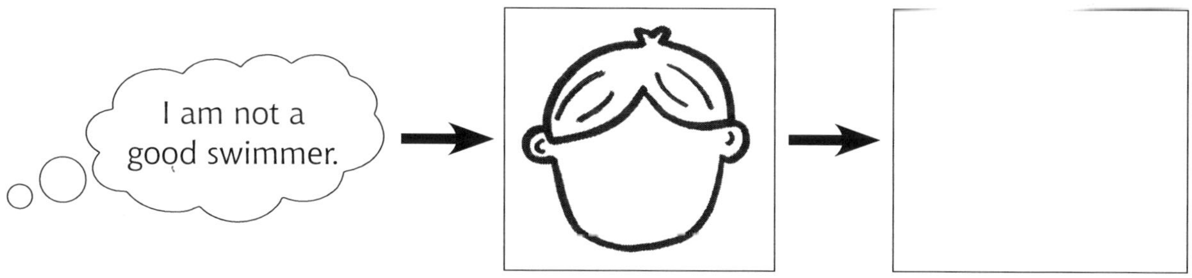

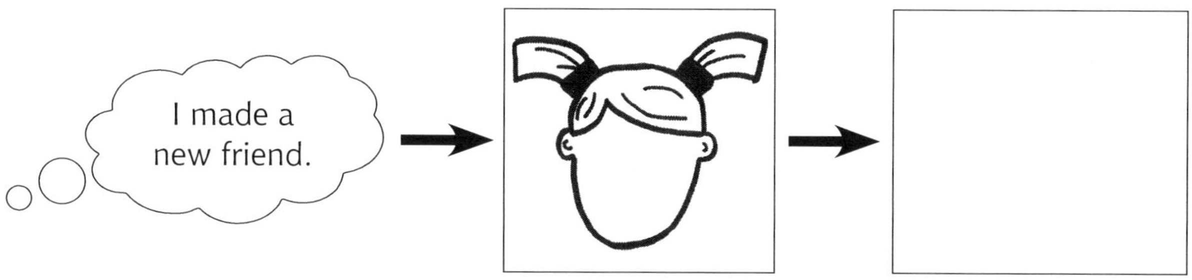

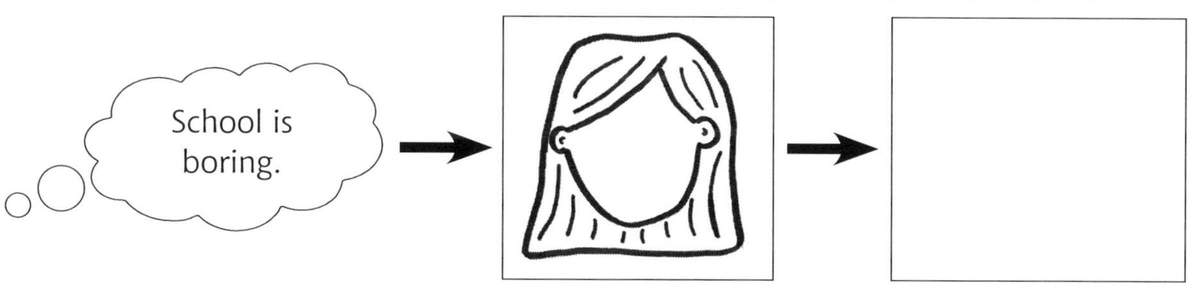

Write a thought of your own and complete the pathway

5. ACTING IN HELPFUL AND UNHELPFUL WAYS

Remember the pathway we spoke about last session? How we think affects how we act. So if we think *helpful* or *unhelpful* thoughts we will act in *helpful* or *unhelpful* ways.

HELPFUL

THOUGHTS

FEELINGS

Confident

ACTIONS

Trying hard and have fun

UNHELPFUL

THOUGHTS

FEELINGS

Disappointed

ACTIONS

Don't try your best

WATCH OUT

Helpful thoughts are *not* just about being positive.

Helpful thoughts are realistic thoughts that help you recognise your strengths and find ways to overcome difficulties to reach your goals.

6. ARE THESE HELPFUL OR UNHELPFUL?

Read the pathways and circle HELPFUL or UNHELPFUL to match the thought, feelings, action pathway.

Everyone else is better than me. → Sad and hopeless → Don't try at anything.

HELPFUL OR UNHELPFUL?

If I try hard I can finish this puzzle. → Determined and hopeful → Don't give up and finish the puzzle.

HELPFUL OR UNHELPFUL?

The new girl is shy, that's why she isn't talking to me. → Friendly and happy → Ask to play with the new girl and make a new friend.

HELPFUL OR UNHELPFUL?

I never win anything. → Frustrated and angry → Do not play games or participate in competitions.

HELPFUL OR UNHELPFUL?

7. HELPFUL THOUGHTS

It is great to increase helpful thoughts.

Here are some I can use:

THESE ARE MY HELPFUL THOUGHTS.

Cut out the *helpful* thoughts and stick them in the thought bubbles on the previous page. Fill in any empty thought bubbles with your own helpful thoughts.

Be careful: not all the thoughts are helpful.

I'm just going to give up.

I have fun even if I don't win.

I will do better next time.

It's too hard.

I always fail and always will.

I have friends who care about me.

Nobody likes me.

I have lots of good qualities

It is OK to ask for help.

I'm not good at it, so why try?

I am a good person.

If I put my mind to it, I can do it.

8. IDENTIFYING WHERE UNHELPFUL THOUGHTS HAPPEN

It is important to know where you have unhelpful thoughts.

Where are two places you have unhelpful thoughts? Replace the unhelpful thoughts with helpful ones and write them in the thought bubbles below.

UNHELPFUL THOUGHT **HELPFUL THOUGHT**

UNHELPFUL THOUGHT **HELPFUL THOUGHT**

9. CONGRATULATE YOURSELF

SELF-HIGH-5

It is important to say congratulations to yourself when you do well, or use helpful thoughts to overcome difficulties.

What is your own way of congratulating yourself?

When can you use it?

....

....

....

10. HOW DOES THIS ALL RELATE TO MY LEARNING?

There are lots of times at school or at home when we have *unhelpful* or *helpful* thoughts, and these shape how well we learn.

What pathways may occur when we are trying to learn something new?

4527 X 763 = ?

UNHELPFUL pathway

I can't do it. → Disappointed and angry with myself → Give up.

HELPFUL pathway

This is tricky, but if I keep trying, then maybe I can get it. → Hopeful → Keep trying.

If I try a different way, maybe I can get it. → Enthusiastic → Keep trying a new way.

If I search for the answer or ask for help, maybe I can get it. → Positive → Keep trying with new information.

11. CAN YOU REPLACE THESE UNHELPFUL THOUGHTS WITH MORE HELPFUL ONES?

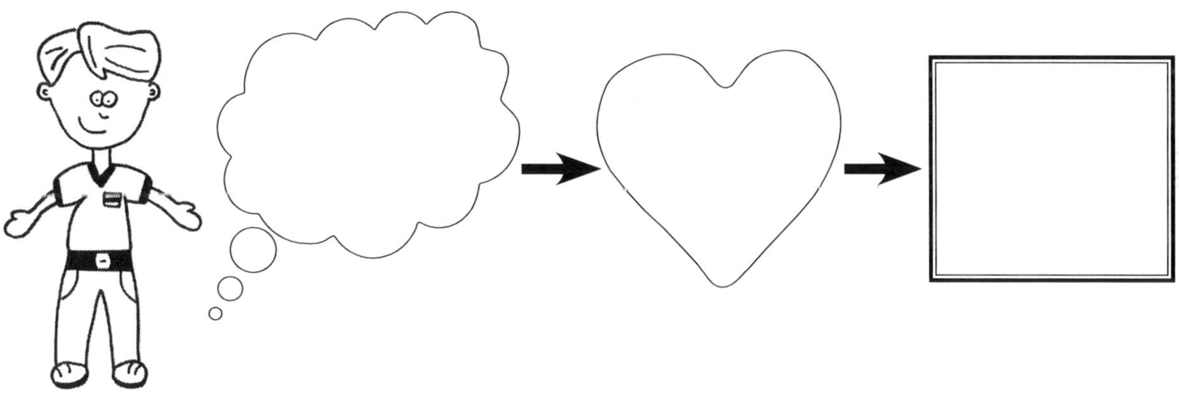

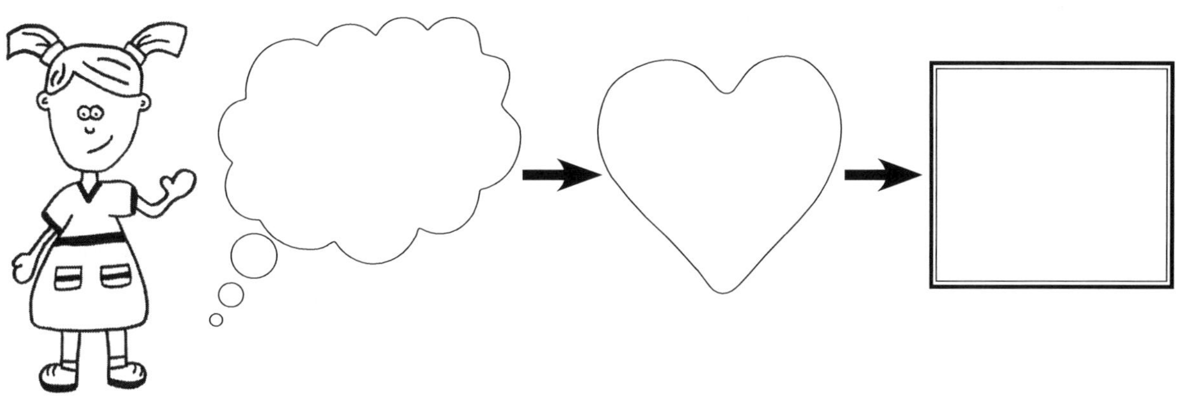

12. SUCCESS AND FAILURE

When we are learning, we are constantly having moments when we feel successful and other moments when we feel like we have failed. These may not be the same for everybody.

What represents success and what represents failure for you?

- I came third in a running race.
- I got half the questions right on a spelling test. This was better than I did last week.
- I finished the maths worksheet, but I was the last in my class to finish.
- I worked really hard on a project and got a C.
- I made a speech in front of the class. It was going really well until I forgot some of the words.
- I was told by the teacher that I was working hard, and other students called me a teacher's pet.
- All the class have started their work, but I didn't understand what to do and just gave up.
- I am placed in the middle group for maths.
- My story came fourth in a writing competition.

13. SUCCESS

Which of these thoughts are *helpful* to think when you achieve success?

(Cross out the *unhelpful* thoughts.)

I tried really hard.

It took me longer to do than the others, so I must be less clever than them.

I asked for help when I had a problem.

It will *never* happen again.

I tried different ways until I found the best one.

It was just easy; that's why I succeeded.

Caution
I was lucky.

If I can do it once, I can do it again.

I am good.

If I can succeed at this then maybe I can succeed at other things as well.

They just let me win because they feel sorry for me.

I can achieve great things if I put my mind to it.

14. FAILURE

Which of these thoughts are *helpful* to think when you feel like you have failed?

(Cross out the *unhelpful* thoughts.)

I *always* fail
and I *always* will.

I only tried one way.
Next time I should
try more.

The teacher hates me.

Caution
I was unlucky.

I didn't try hard
enough. If I try harder
next time I will do it.

It just shows that
I am not clever.

When I had a problem,
I didn't ask for help.

Everyone fails
sometimes.

If I can't do this,
I probably can't do
a lot of things.

I can't be the best
at everything, and
that's OK.

Everyone now thinks
that I am not clever.

I gave up when it
became hard. Next time
I shouldn't give up so
quickly.

15. WHY?

Give a possible reason why the following events occurred using only *helpful* thoughts.

You can use examples of reasons listed on the previous pages or make up your own.

You get the highest mark in the class on a maths test.

WHY? ....

You do not read your book before your presentation for book week.

WHY? ....

You are the only one in the class who hasn't finished the science project.

WHY? ....

You answer the hard question correctly in front of the class.

WHY? ....

16. BECOMING A SUPERHERO

Super Powers to Stop Unhelpful Thoughts

It is not always easy to stop unhelpful thoughts. You are going to be given three *super powers* to help you fight off unhelpful thoughts and become a **SUPERHERO**!

THE SUPER POWERS

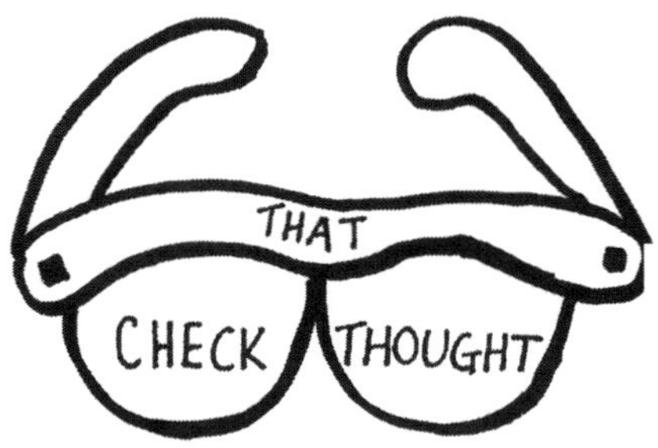

17. SUPER POWER #1

HOW TO **STOP** THAT **THOUGHT:**

18. THE POWER OF STOP THAT THOUGHT

19. SUPER POWER # 2

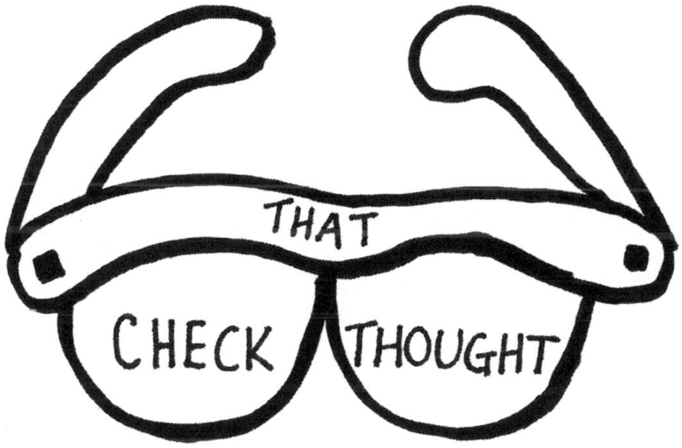

HOW TO **CHECK** THAT **THOUGHT:**

20. THE POWER OF CHECK THAT THOUGHT

21. SUPER POWER # 3

HOW TO **CHANGE** THAT **THOUGHT:**

22. THE POWER OF CHANGE THAT THOUGHT

23. OUR SUPER POWERS

WHAT ARE THE THREE SUPER POWERS?

THAT THOUGHT	THAT THOUGHT	THAT THOUGHT

WHY DO WE HAVE THEM?

WHEN CAN WE USE THEM?

24. ROLE-PLAYS

SAVING OTHERS FROM UNHELPFUL THOUGHTS

- You are learning about fractions in maths, but you just don't understand what a fraction is.

  'I'm just not good at maths and never will be.'

- Your teacher says that the three best students in the class will be given a special treat. You work really hard but you're not chosen.

  'Why should I work hard if the teacher doesn't even notice?'

- Your class goes to the pool; you are the only one who cannot swim.

  'Everyone is going to laugh at me.'

- You come fifth in a running race.

  'I'm so slow.'

- For a project you make a model of Earth. When you bring yours to school you see that your friends' projects are better than yours.

  'My work is never as good as my friends.'

- In maths you can't remember your eight times table.

  'Everyone else can do it. I'm the worst in the class.'

- The music teacher asks you to clap a beat, but you get it wrong.

  'I hate music.'

- Your friends are all reading books that are more difficult than yours.

  'I can't read well and never will.'

25. ROLE-PLAYS

SAVING YOURSELF FROM UNHELPFUL THOUGHTS

- The teacher gives you a story to read, but you don't understand some of the words.
- You have to give a speech in front of the class but you are scared.
- In art you are making clay sculptures, but yours breaks.
- Your teacher asks the class a question. You put up your hand but you say the wrong answer.
- On a spelling test you get all of the words wrong.
- You are the only one in your class who has not done the home-learning task.

26. DEFEATING THE EVIL MONSTERS

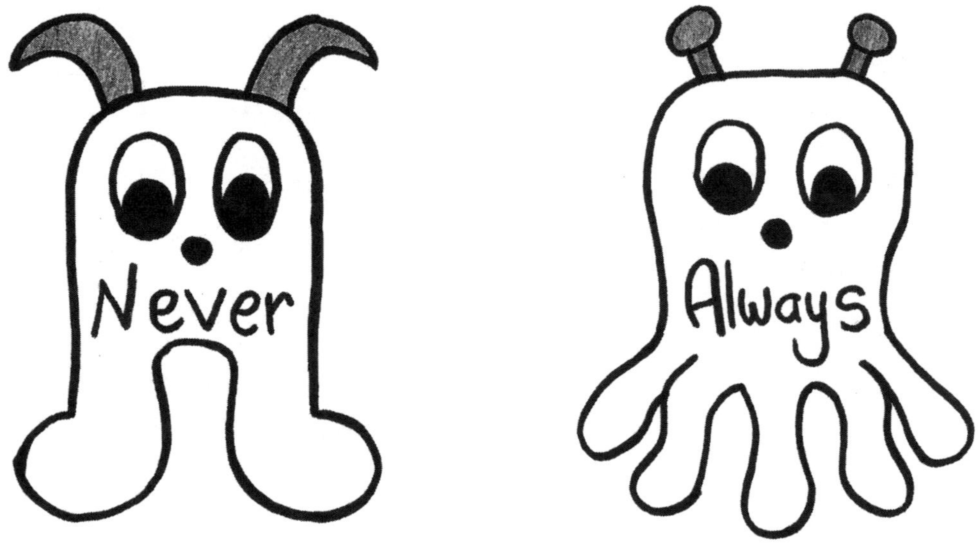

Why are these monsters bad?

How can we defeat them?

27. EVERYTHING WE HAVE LEARNT

Are you confident that you have learnt the answers to these questions?

☐ How are thoughts, feelings and actions linked?

☐ What is the difference between *helpful* and *unhelpful* thoughts?

☐ Why are *unhelfpul* thoughts unhelpful?

☐ How do our thoughts impact our learning?

☐ What should I do if I succeed or do something well?

☐ What are some helpful thoughts to explain *why* I did well?

☐ What are some helpful thoughts to explain *why* I did not do as well as I would like?

☐ Why should I try to defeat the unhelpful thoughts?

☐ How can I defeat the unhelpful thoughts?

☐ I *can* think *helpful thoughts* and use all these skills to help my learning.

28. SETTING GOALS FOR MY LEARNING

Where do you think you are *now* with your achievements at school?

Draw yourself on the staircase.

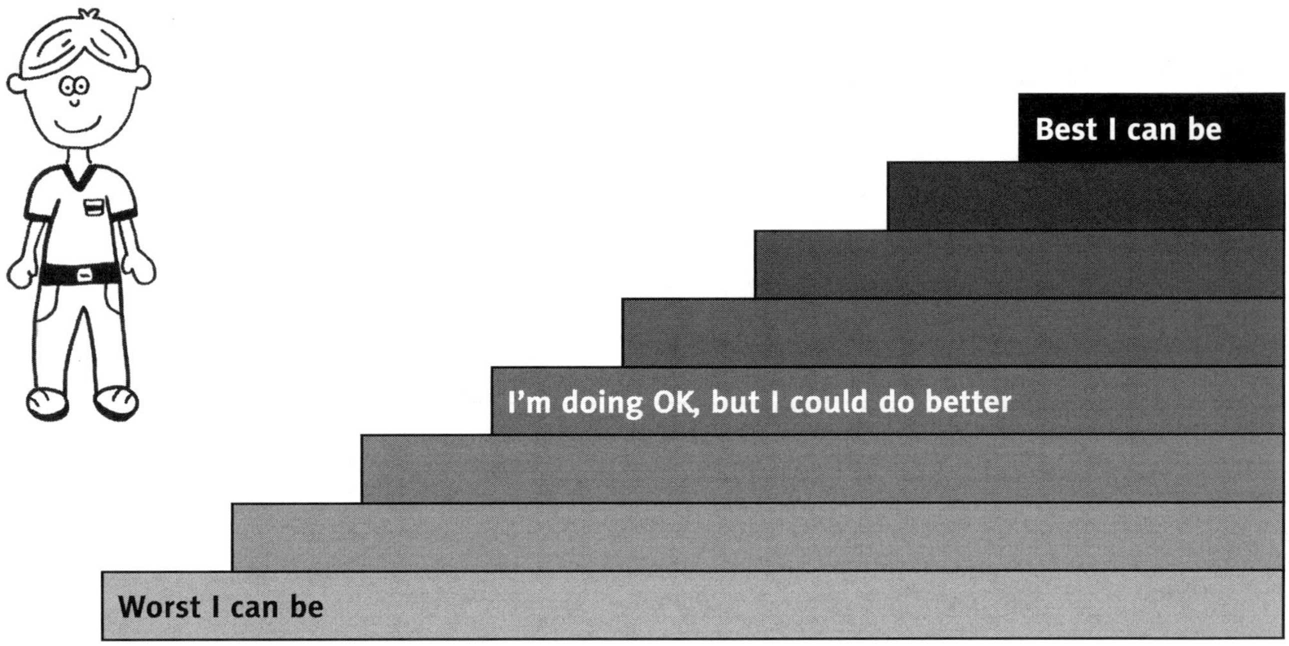

Where do you *want to be* with your achievements at school?

Draw yourself on the staircase.

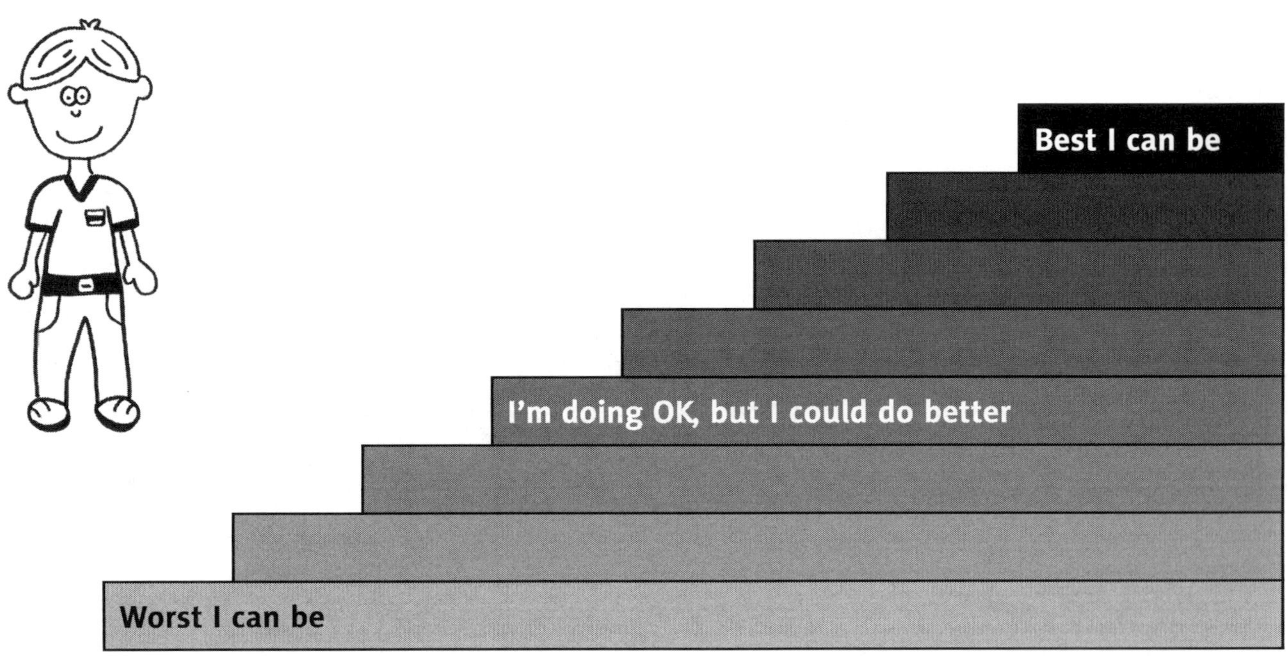

HOME-LEARNING WORKSHEETS

ACTIVITIES TO PRACTISE WHAT YOU HAVE LEARNT

CAN YOU GUESS THE THOUGHT?

Watch someone do something and try to guess what he or she was feeling and thinking. You can ask the person what he or she was thinking to check if you guessed right.

Action you saw:	Feeling?	Thought?

What did they really feel and think?

Action you saw:	Feeling?	Thought?

What did they really feel and think?

PLEASE BRING ME TO SCHOOL ON THIS DAY: ____________________

ACTIVITIES TO PRACTISE WHAT YOU HAVE LEARNT

IS MY THINKING HELPFUL?

Fill in 1 *helpful* and 1 *unhelpful* thought–feeling–action pathway based on your experience *or* make one up.

Also think of some more helpful thoughts that we can add to our Helpful Thoughts page.

I HAD A HELPFUL THOUGHT

I HAD AN UNHELPFUL THOUGHT

HELPFUL THOUGHTS

PLEASE BRING ME TO SCHOOL ON THIS DAY: ______________________

ACTIVITIES TO PRACTICE WHAT YOU HAVE LEARNT

WHERE DO I HAVE HELPFUL AND UNHELPFUL THOUGHTS?

Fill in below about what helpful and unhelpful thoughts you have and where they happen.

HELPFUL THOUGHT

The thought: ______________________

Where I had the thought: ______________________

What I was doing when I had the thought: ______________________

UNHELPFUL THOUGHT

The thought: ______________________

Where I had the thought: ______________________

What I was doing when I had the thought: ______________________

WHERE DO I USE SELF-CONGRATULATIONS?

UNHELPFUL THOUGHT

Where I used my self-congratulations: ______________________

What I had done: ______________________

What I thought: ______________________

PLEASE BRING ME TO SCHOOL ON THIS DAY: ______________________

ACTIVITIES TO PRACTISE WHAT YOU HAVE LEARNT

MAKING A BOOK ABOUT HELPFUL THINKING

It is your turn to make a storybook that shows helpful thoughts and how to use them.

For example, remember the book we looked at in class.

PLEASE BRING ME TO SCHOOL ON THIS DAY: ______________________

ACTIVITIES TO PRACTISE WHAT YOU HAVE LEARNT

EXPLAINING WHY YOU SUCCEED AND FAIL

Fill out the sheet about a time this week when you have felt success and failure.

SUCCESS

What I did to make me feel successful: ______________________

My thought – why I succeeded: ______________________

____

If the thought was unhelpful, can you replace it with a more helpful one?
My helpful thought: ______________________

____

FAILURE

What I did to make me feel failure: ______________________

My thought – why I failed: ______________________

____

If the thought was unhelpful, can you replace it with a more helpful one?
My helpful thought: ______________________

____

PLEASE BRING ME TO SCHOOL ON THIS DAY: ______________________

ACTIVITIES TO PRACTISE WHAT YOU HAVE LEARNT

MAKING A COMIC STRIP TO TELL THE STORY OF

YOUR SUPERHERO

USING THE THREE SUPER POWERS

TO DEFEAT THE ENEMY

UNHELPFUL THOUGHTS

COMIC STRIP STORY – PLAN:

Who is the superhero? ....

Where is the story set? ....

Who is in trouble and why? ....

What unhelpful thoughts are they having? ....

What super powers will you use? ....

What will happen next? ....

PLEASE BRING ME TO SCHOOL ON THIS DAY: ____________________

ACTIVITIES TO PRACTISE WHAT YOU HAVE LEARNT

BEING A SUPERHERO IN THE REAL WORLD

Practise using the three super powers at school or at home. Write down an example of one of these times for each of the super powers.

What was the unhelpful thought? ______________________________

How did you defeat it? ______________________________

What was the unhelpful thought? ______________________________

How did you defeat it? ______________________________

What was the unhelpful thought? ______________________________

How did you defeat it? ______________________________

DRAW YOURSELF AS A SUPER HERO

PLEASE BRING ME TO SCHOOL ON THIS DAY: ______________________________

EXTRA MATERIAL

EMOTION FACE CARDS

EMOTION LABELS

HOPEFUL
BORED
SURPRISED
DISGUSTED
CONFIDENT
ANGRY
FRUSTRATED
ANXIOUS
SAD
HAPPY

THOUGHT PATHWAYS

We are going to lose our basketball game. → Sad and hopeless → Don't practise basketball or try in your basketball game.

I've worked hard on my picture and it's good. → Proud and happy → Show other people your picture and draw more pictures.

I can be whatever I want when I grow up.
Confident and excited
Working hard in school.

I can't sing; my voice is really bad.
Embarrassed and disappointed
Never sing.

I am always left out of the game.
Sad and alone
Sit alone at lunchtime.

If I ask them then maybe they will want to play with me.
Hopeful and optimistic
Make friends and play games together.

When I ask nicely I usually get what I want.
Optimistic and confident
Ask your parents for what you want.

I'm never allowed to do what I want.
Angry and frustrated
Yell at your parents.

Nothing is going right today.
Frustrated and angry
Stop trying with anything.

I'm having a great day.
Happy
You are kind and friendly to others.

I love playing video games.

Excited and glad

Play video games with your brother and have fun.

School is boring.

Frustrated and bored

Pretend you are sick so you don't have to go to school.

I did well in my test; I think I can do well in my next test as well. → Proud and hopeful → Keep working hard for the next test.

I hate myself. → Disappointed and sad → Don't make an effort to do fun activities or make friends.

I can run faster than lots of people. → Confident and proud → Enter into the school running competition.

This question is too complicated. → Confused and frustrated → Give up on the question.

I made a new friend today. → Happy → Make plans to do something with your new friend.

No one likes my jokes. → Embarrassed → Stop making jokes and being yourself.

HELPFUL TARGET

UNHELPFUL TARGET

QUESTION CARDS

CAN YOU PAT YOUR HEAD AND RUB YOUR TUMMY AT THE SAME TIME?
CAN YOU JUMP ON ONE LEG FOR 30 SECONDS WITHOUT FALLING OVER?
CAN YOU TOUCH YOUR NOSE WITH YOUR TONGUE?
CAN YOU DO THE SPLITS?
CAN YOU TOUCH THE CEILING?

WHAT IS THE CAPITAL CITY OF ENGLAND?

Answer: London

WHAT IS THE CAPITAL CITY OF SWITZERLAND?

Answer: Bern

AT WHAT TEMPERATURE DOES WATER BOIL?

Answer: 100°C or 212°F

WHAT YEAR DID WORLD WAR 2 END?

Answer: 1945

WHO WAS A FAMOUS QUEEN OF EGYPT?

Answer: Cleopatra

READ:

GREAT

READ:

ENGLISH

READ:

ANAESTHETIC

READ:

OTORHINOLARYNGOLOGICAL

WHAT IS THE MODE OF THESE NUMBERS?
3, 6, 8, 9, 0, 6

SPELL:

FIREMAN

SPELL:

FANTASTIC

SPELL:

PSYCHOLOGY

SPELL:

ARCHAEOLOGICAL

ORDER THESE NUMBERS FROM SMALLEST TO LARGEST:
576, 298, 318, 592

Answer: 298, 318, 576, 592

WHAT IS THE ANSWER?

22 + 22

Answer: 44

WHAT IS THE ANSWER?

97.75230 – 15.643

Answer: 82.1093

WHAT IS THE ANSWER?

5 X 5

Answer: 25

WHAT IS THE ANSWER?

629 X 24

Answer: 15,096

WHAT IS THE ANSWER?

(√) 100

Answer: 10

BELIEVING YOU CAN IS THE FIRST STEP TO ACHIEVING

LOVE
I ~~HATE~~ MATHS

Alicia Chodkiewicz

Lucy loved school.

She loved painting in art

and playing instruments in music

and reading books in the library.

But one thing about school that Lucy hated was...

MATHS

She found maths hard,

she didn't often get the right answers,

and she got low grades.

LUCY THOUGHT:

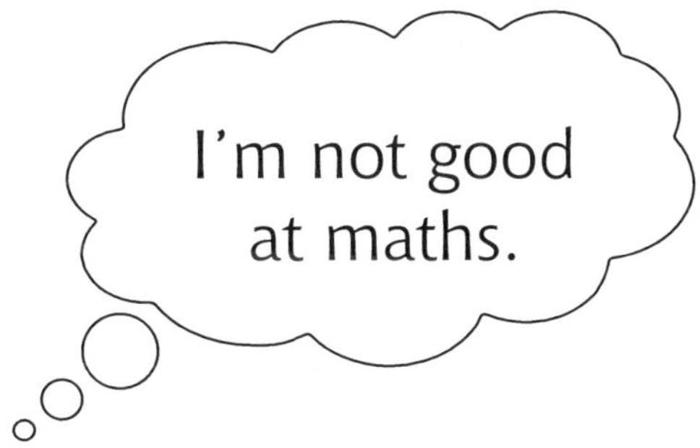

LUCY FELT:

sad, hopeless and unmotivated.

LUCY DID:

not try in class

and did not do her maths home-learning.

One day the teacher was worried about Lucy.

She told Lucy that it is important to think *helpful* thoughts about maths because

The next day, Lucy decided to use a helpful thought in maths.

LUCY THOUGHT:

LUCY FELT:

happy, hopeful and motivated.

LUCY DID:

try in class, even on tricky questions.

She did not always get the questions correct, but the more she tried, the more she got right.

Lucy also began to do all her maths home-learning.

The more helpful thoughts Lucy had,

the more effort she made in maths

and the more her maths skills and grades improved.

At the end of the year the teacher asked Lucy:

LUCY REPLIED:

I love painting in art,

I love playing instruments in music,

I love reading books in the library

and

I LOVE MATHS.

UNDERSTANDING ACTIONS

What was happening around you at the time this happened?

What was your action?

What did you feel before you did this action?

What thought did you have to make you feel this way?

What was happening around you at the time this happened?

What was your action?

What did you feel before you did this action?

What thought did you have to make you feel this way?

EVALUATING THOUGHTS POSTER

Is your thought:

HELPFUL THOUGHTS POSTER

EXPLAINING *WHY*?

WHAT IS THE EVENT?

DO YOU FEEL: Success / Failure?

WHY DO YOU THINK THE EVENT OCCURRED?

IS THE REASON: Helpful / Unhelpful?

IF THE REASON IS UNHELPFUL, WHAT IS A MORE HELPFUL REASON?

SUPER POWERS POSTER

THIS CERTIFICATE IS AWARDED TO

....

For successfully completing the programme

BELIEVING YOU CAN
IS THE FIRST STEP TO
ACHIEVING

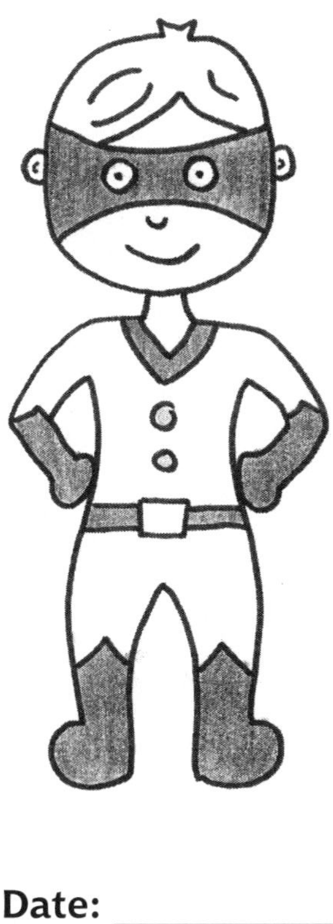

You are now a certified

SUPER HERO

with the power to defeat

UNHELPFUL THOUGHTS

Date: ________________

Instructor's signature: ____________________________